THE FIRST BOOK OF SAINTS: TEN PROFILES IN MISSION

Edited by Dean Salter

Sponsored by the Committee on Education
for Mission and published by:

THE   UNITED   CHURCH

PUBLISHING   HOUSE

ISBN 0-91900045-2

Publisher: R.L. Naylor
Editor: Dean Salter
Production Editor: Lynda Walton

Cover design and portraits: Robert Hoffmann

THE FIRST BOOK OF SAINTS: TEN PROFILES IN MISSION

Let justice roll on like a river and righteousness like an ever-flowing stream. (Amos 5:24)

CONTENTS

PREFACE

"*The First Book of Saints*? What kind of a title is that? We don't have saints in our church!" That's the kind of reaction I received when I told people what we were going to call this book. At first blush, it does seem like an odd title for a book that deals primarily with United Church members. Certainly, the outstanding people who are profiled in the following pages don't consider themselves saints, at least not in the exalted way the word is most commonly used. They're not ready to have anyone put the word "saint" in front of their first names.

So why is this *The First Book of Saints*? Biblically, the saints were all those who made the courageous step of joining the Christian Church (N.T.) and/or who acted out their lives as loyal servants of their God (N.T. and O.T.). That's a much broader, more inclusive concept of saints than most of us seem to have today. It's this type of "saint" that we're profiling here: dedicated, delightful, dynamic members of the communion of saints, to which we all belong. The ten people you'll learn about in this book are saints. But, they're saints under the same terms of grace and personal commitment that allow you and me to call ourselves saints as well.

This book has been created under the theory that one of the best ways to equip, enable and energize the saints is to learn about the faithful journeys of our brother and sister saints. The United Church's national Committee on Education for Mission believes very strongly in the power of personal stories. It was this committee who commissioned *The First Book of Saints* as one way of showing the dynamic attitudes and actions which some of the saints are bringing to the church's mission. Today, with the invaluable support of the United Church Publishing House, this book is in your hands as both an educational guide and a challenge.

A challenge? Yes, a challenge. When we eventually do the second, third, fourth and fifth *Book of Saints* we want you to do more than read other people's stories in them. We want there to be a chapter about you.

— —*Dean Salter*

STELLA BURRY:
SOCIAL SERVICE PIONEER

by B. Gail Weir

Dr. Stella Burry's life's work has been as a diaconal minister with The United Church of Canada. The first 12 years of that work were done in Toronto and the remainder have been carried out in St. John's, Newfoundland. She's now 90 years of age and she's still working to meet the needs of others. The emphasis of her work today is on the aged as she attempts to help the elderly who wish to remain independent of institutions. Born Stella Annie Burry on August 11, 1897, she says, "I'm a Leo. If I make up my mind to do something, I'll do it."

Stella is proud of her heritage. The community of Greenspond, an island in Bonavista Bay on Newfoundland's northeast coast, was a thriving centre of the fishing and sealing industries when she was a child growing up there. It boasted a population of almost 2,000 people and was known locally as "The Capital of the North". Says Stella, "I think they were wonderful people, not that they were perfect. They were humble people. Fishermen couldn't be proud. They were hard workers and they were never sure of the future. The fisherman had to walk into the merchant's office with his cap in his hand."

"I thank the Lord for the first five years of my life. I mean, what I've got, it came down through my grandparents and the church and the Sunday Schools." Stella can remember her grandfather and his old yellow Bible — how he would take her on his knee and show her the big letters. "He was an Anglican and he trotted me to church every Sunday morning, to the Church of England church." As the family grew, they had to move out of her mother's family home and into the unused half of her grandfather Burry's house. With that switch she also switched to the Methodist Church and school.

Stella was the eldest of four children. Her father was a fisherman and her mother earned extra money for the family by curing fish brought back by the fishermen who went to Labrador and the Straits of Belle Isle to fish in the summertime. Stella says, "A fisherman's wife is always sure to be a working woman, she doesn't take it easy." Her mother earned 20 cents for curing or "making" each quintal of fish and, in order to help with the cost of school books, "we would have to be on the flake with her." A quintal consisted of 112 pounds and "making" the fish was the term used for the salting process. The salted fish was laid out on the "flakes" which were platforms made of unpainted poles. "We'd wash it first. She'd put on her oil-skin apron and she'd wash it. Then we'd get it up to the flake. If the rain came, we'd have to hurry to cover it."

There was no free education in those days and her mother drilled it into Stella and her sister that they were going to be educated. They were not going to be maids. This was the fate of the majority of young girls who worked like slaves for little more than their room and board. "My mother was always working for my good."

As a child, Stella was greatly influenced by the visiting missionaries. "In our Methodist Church we had a wonderful missionary meeting once a year. I can't remember all of them, but I know I was very much impressed with the man telling about the missionaries being needed in Japan. And then, the next year, we had Dr. Service from China who showed us the 'magic lantern' (slides of his work). That settled me."

Her own minister, the Reverend Ezra Broughton, a Methodist minister from England, heard of her interest in mission and encouraged it by lending her some books. Later, he asked her if she would like to be a deaconess. She didn't know what that was and he explained that it was a woman who visits the poor and the sick and helps people. He showed her pictures of deaconesses at work. "There they were with the most angelic faces, those women, with little blue caps and those nice white strings, bows hanging down."

In a Sunday School library book she read about something called "The Whatsoever Band". She was 12 or 13 at the time. "And so I organized a Whatsoever Band, got going an organization when I was that age and got a group of girls around me and we went around amongst the poor. We did things for the old and the poor. I think I caught from my mother her great sympathy for the sick and poor people." Aunt Carey, as her mother was known, was called from her bed many nights to go to the aid of sick neighbours.

Rev. Broughton recognized Stella's special qualities. She says he told her to "'Come to the prayer meetings and take part. Practice. Don't be afraid to give a testimony, don't be afraid to make a prayer.' Real Methodist stuff. And, I may say that I made my Christian decision and I didn't make it in an evangelistic meeting. But, I made it. I stood up and said that I wanted to live my life for Jesus Christ in a girls' meeting in old Greenspond."

She had a strict school teacher, Mr. E.J. Crummey, and she credits his discipline with getting her successfully through the public exams. The summer before her final year of school, while visiting an aunt in St. John's, she met her first deaconess and did some visiting with her. Stella was, of course, moved by someone who was living out her own dream. But, because of the expense involved, going away to Toronto for diaconal training was out of the question.

In 1914, following secondary school, she went to St. John's for six weeks of summer school, where specialists were brought together by the various churches to instruct in teaching methods. At this time, she saw teaching as her only possibility for work. "You could be a maid. And mother had made up her mind that her daughters were not going to be maids. She knew she couldn't send us to college, which made us feel very humble. And I didn't want to go behind a counter and measure off stuff and handle groceries and so on. I think her mind was set on my being a teacher."

Stella taught in several Newfoundland communities over a period of eight years. It was near the end of this time that she almost decided to marry, which would have meant an end to her dreams of becoming a deaconess. It was a difficult time for her and she got through it by praying to God for guidance. When she received a message that she was needed to teach in another part of the province, she knew what her choice had to be. "The worst thing of all was hurting the man but, you know, he found somebody after all."

She taught for one more year before applying to the

Methodist National Training School, which is now called the Centre for Christian Studies. Then, with $550 that she had saved over the years from her annual salary of $140, she headed for Toronto. This was quite a big step for her and she received no encouragement from family and friends, who must have thought it unusual that she had not settled down to the traditional role of wife and mother by now.

The training school was a large building at the corner of St. Clair and Avenue Road. Deaconesses who worked in the city were living there. "They were flitting around in their uniforms, their white cuffs and collars and they had taken up hats by that time. The white ties were no longer going." It was also a home for missionaries on leave to do further study. Rev. Hiram Hull was the principal during Stella's first year. She remembers being called into his office, where he showed her the proper way to bow on entering the dining room and, "forever after I bowed graciously." She headed the class that year and won the Timothy Eaton prize of $100. "I was a poor, ignorant Newfoundlander who didn't know much, but had a keen mind as it happened."

It was about this time that she attended the inaugural service of The United Church of Canada. Wearing her navy uniform with its stiff white collar, she lined up on Mutual Street to get into the arena. She recalls that the cuffs seemed to be very, very hot, but the occasion was worth the discomfort. "I can never express the solemnity of that wonderful service and I will never forget the communion as we communed together."

In her second year, the principal was Dr. Winnifred Thomas, who gave her the choice of either majoring in Christian education or social work. She remembers thinking, "Well, I can get Christian education from now on, but I won't get the training in sociology. Now, while I've got the chance, I'll go." The training school was affiliated with the School of Social Work of Victoria University. There she studied counselling, as well as children's needs, and did some field work. Her advisor in her second year was Dr. Peter Bryce, who was running what was called the Neighbourhood Workers in Toronto. He later became Moderator of The United Church of Canada. "He was a Scotsman, one of God's gracious gentlemen. He always wore a rose." As graduation approached, she had to decide whether to serve in an institution or work in the community. "He said to me, 'Stella, your work is in the community. That is where you will do it.' "

She was assigned to Woodbine Methodist Church, which was out in the country. Dr. Bryce was the minister there. "He could walk into a room and get all kinds of money and (consequently) a wealthy lady paid my salary for four years. I was asked to do ever so many things that I thought I never could do: run the prayer meeting and do so many other things." He was trying to build up the congregation so he had Stella carry out a survey, going up and down the roads, knocking on doors. "I made a special effort to talk to the mothers. Nobody turned me down. I didn't know what church they belonged to."

After four years at Woodbine, she was called to Carlton United which had been slated to close its doors. Dr. E. Crossley Hunter had come down from North Bay to be the minister at the old church. The doors were supposed to be locked because the congregation had moved out to other parts of the city and the Board felt the church could no longer support itself. These were the Depression years and about a fifth of the population of Toronto was on the welfare roles. Dr. Hunter put a sign on the door which said "House of Friendship" and, with Stella's help, the whole situation turned around. She called on young women living in the downtown apartments and boarding houses and got them to come from the hospitals and other institutions to the rejuvenated church. They held meetings after church and on week nights to discuss ways to help the needy.

She had a room at the church where she counselled. She also had a Sunday School class and a Business Girls' Club. The club met on Thursday nights and was designed for young girls who had come to Toronto to find work. A lot of them were from the east and from out in the country. (When Stella returned to Toronto for a visit in 1986, she had a reunion with eight of the club's original members.)

Stella also spent much time visiting young mothers. She would sit and chat and drink numerous cups of tea with them, anywhere from 14 to 30 cups a day. (She has credited the tea with giving her the stamina needed to keep up her gruelling pace.) "There's no trouble to get close to people, my dear. Some of them needed a bit of warming. My mother was a favourite with people and I suppose I took after her and I took after my father's strength, I suppose, in some other ways."

Recalling her efforts to know the spiritual as well as the physical needs of the poor makes her think of today's food banks. Stella doesn't agree with the concept of simply passing out food. "We're just feeding them and that's all we're doing. In this society, we've got to do more than feed people. It's the important thing, I know, but it's not the *only* important thing. If we're going to give ourselves as a church, let's *give* ourselves, our *whole* selves; give every bit of what we've got to give, what the Lord has given us."

Stella has lived by this premise herself. While at Carlton United, she would sleep all day Saturday to make up for lost rest during the week. "I've overworked all my life. There was no normal working day. I'd get up in the mornings and I never thought about hours. Look at our Lord. He never thought about hours."

After ten years working at this rate, Stella was feeling very tired. Dr. Bryce asked her to come down to Metropolitan United where he was then serving, but she heard of another opening that was more appealing to her. She met Mission Superintendent Dr. Oliver Jackson, who told her that he had applied to the Home Mission Board for money to put a social worker in St. John's. They didn't have the funds but had, in turn, asked the Woman's Missionary Society, who agreed to provide the worker. They had originally intended to send Stella's friend, Bess French, but Bess felt her work was with the native people. Dr. Thomas of the training school was now executive secretary of the Society and, because Stella knew her well, she approached her about the position and told her that she'd like to go. Dr. Thomas told her, "We'll see, Stella. If we can't find anyone else, we'll send you." Stella replied, "Whoever goes, Dr. Thomas, it's my job." "That was how strongly I felt the call back," she says now. "I could have gone (to Metropolitan) and had a much easier life and easier work."

In September, 1938 she began her work in St. John's in the empty rooms of the Old Star Building on the corner of Adelaide and New Gower streets. She started by asking local ministers who the poor people were. Not satisfied with their response, she went to the welfare office, which listed welfare recipients according to religious denomination.

It seemed too impersonal to her merely to place an ad in the paper announcing that the office was open. Instead, armed with a list of 222 names, she set out that first fall to visit all the families on the list. "We clothed, that first winter, 275 children and got them to school. I visited homes where there weren't enough knives and forks, weren't enough dishes, where women didn't have coats to wear."

Stella organized 40 volunteers from the city's four United Churches into the Community Service League and soon her empty rooms were buzzing with activity. Before very long, there were three sewing classes, plus instruction in health, nutrition and cooking. "I felt we had to build up the self-worth of people and so it became really a house of friendship."

She started a buying club which developed into a credit union, the only co-operative women's credit union in Newfoundland at that time. She also initiated a Parents' Association which became Newfoundland's first United Church Home and School Association. Then World War II started and generated even more work.

Stella organized summer schools where the underprivileged participated in recreational activities while receiving Christian and cultural education. She also helped set up a summer school camp at the Jackson-Walsh Memorial Camp in Western Bay, dedicated to the memory of Dr. Oliver Jackson. She put a great deal of energy into establishing summer camps and obtaining a permanent campground at Shoe Cove near St. John's. In recognition of this work, the latter site was named Burry Heights in her honour by Mrs. C. Loveys, the Woman's Missionary Society Home Missions Executive Secretary, on a field trip to Newfoundland in 1948.

Along with all this work, Stella made time on Sunday afternoons to visit the sanatorium where tuberculosis cases were treated. "As I look back over it now, I wonder how I ever got the strength to do what I did." Again, as in Toronto, she kept no regular hours. "And I had ten dollars a month for expenses, for my personal expenses. That's what the Board offered me, so I didn't have very much."

In 1944, she received a deaconess grant to go to the College of Theology in New York to study Christian education and counselling for the summer. While there, she was able to observe some of the social work programs that were being carried out. Something that interested her greatly was the "settlement house" concept in which group activities were conducted on the first floor while the upper floors were a residence for people with special needs. She thought of how, during the war, girls from the outports had often come to her for help in getting boarding houses. Rooms were scarce because of the American presence in St. John's. Now it occurred to her that a settlement house would be a good way to help these girls while still carrying on the church's social work. She had no way of knowing that in just a few years she would be running such a home.

Activities at the community centre came to an abrupt halt when the building burned down on January 28, 1945. Stella recalls going there the next day and looking through a large hole that was burned in the wall. She could see the Southside Hills beyond and she said to herself, "Lord, well this is over. Lord, there must be something else for us."

When the war ended, a house that had been run as a respite centre by Canadian YWCA War Services for girls serving in the war came up for sale. The house was perfect for Stella's needs because there was space on the lower floors for the office and group work while the upper two floors could be used as a girls' residence. A committee of laypeople from the four United Churches raised the money to secure the property and the Woman's Missionary Society provided a maintenance grant. They named it United Church House.

Because the house was old, it was in need of repairs and there was still money owing on the mortgage in 1951. Once again, the WMS came through, but it was on the condition that the house be named for a church that was closing its doors in Montreal. Money from the sale of the church was used to pay off the debts on what was now going to be called Emmanuel House.

Stella can't say enough in praise of the work done by church women. "I think the women have been very, very valuable to the church. And that's one sample of it. When the women set out for anything, they'll get there. They find ways to do things. Their feet don't stop. They'll do it with their feet; they'll do it with their brains; they'll do it somehow."

On September 1, 1964, Stella retired from her official duties as deaconess and community worker but in no way did she retire from the work of God. She actually continued to serve on the staff of Emmanuel House until 1968. In 1965, she served her second term as a member of the General Council Executive, representing Newfoundland Conference. She has been a member of presbytery and Conference for more than 40 years. In 1967, Stella agreed to organize voluntary services to the Waterford Hospital for Mental and Nervous Diseases. She co-ordinated the visiting and women's services of the church. The St. John's Jaycees named her Citizen of the Year for 1967 because of this work, but also in appreciation of her ongoing contribution to the city's social work. In 1971, the honorary degree, Doctor of Divinity, was bestowed on her by the Atlantic School of Theology in Halifax, recognizing her dedication to the social service work of the United Church.

Aside from her work at the Community Centre and Emmanuel House, Stella was heavily involved with the United Church Children's Home on Hamilton Avenue. When the provincial government closed down this home she "fought quite a battle and got into a lot of hot water" in her efforts to establish a group home for the older children. She was on the committee that purchased the new group home and fixed it up.

Stella's contributions to her city and province have been enormous. She was a founding member and served on the Board of the Community Services Council, established in 1975 to co-ordinate community services and assist voluntary associations. She served for many years on the Housing Authority of the Public Housing Service. She was on the committee that promoted the Agnes Pratt Home for the Aged, which opened in 1958, and she has been on the Home's governing board ever since. At age 82, Stella stepped down as Executive President of the Newfoundland and Labrador Association for the Aging, an educational and advisory organization. While in this position, she spent a great deal of time drawing up the bylaws. She also took part in seminars and conferences on aging and spoke to Memorial University medical students on the needs of the elderly.

Now at age 90, Stella Burry is no longer physically able to get out and do the leg work for the projects that need her attention. "I've been racing around all my life," she says. "I never stopped. Somebody always needed me." She still lives in her own home in the center of St. John's. Her good neighbours and many friends come by to give a hand with various chores. She's thankful for the many volunteers who give her a few hours of their time and says, "My church has been good to me."

She still works on a committee for the aging. "I'm trying to help them see that there's no let-up in Christian service." In 1986, she travelled to Toronto, where she made a special effort to visit group homes for the aged. She feels strongly that the able-bodied elderly should not have to move into institutions where everything is done for them. An ideal situation would be group homes where six to eight people could share responsibilities and maintain some of their independence. She, herself, spent some time in an institution a few years ago when she broke her leg, but moved back into her own home as soon as she was strong enough so that someone who really needed it could have the bed.

Stella believes that the church's mission is laid out quite clearly in the teachings of the Scriptures. "I think the people that want to know and are sincere in it, they may make mistakes, but they will do God's work. If we ask every day for His guidance, the Holy Spirit works." She has followed this dictate all her life and has no regrets. "I'm in His vineyard and — you know the story of the people who went in late to the vineyard and were accepted — I feel that I'm accepted now. I think the Lord must be using me a little bit. I'm quite sure He does."

CHAPTER 2

CLAUDE DE MESTRAL: ACTIVIST, PASTOR AND POLITICIAN

by Daniel Fines

He may be over 80, but he still speaks with the enthusiasm of a young man ready to take on any challenge. Rev. Claude de Mestral has roamed five continents and immersed himself in a wide variety of social battles. Along the way, he has tried to build bridges between people—between different cultures and religious groups. Never one to be stopped by official structures, his long, faithful ministry in the United Church has been far from tranquil. In private, many a parishioner must have questioned the ways of this unique pastor who was a committed social activist even before French Canada went through the reforms of the 1960s.

Claude was born to a French family at the beginning of the century in a part of Switzerland that had more missionaries abroad than ministers at home. His mother's family, forced to flee Catholic France two centuries before, had a long history of producing Protestant ministers. So, in addition to his clergyman father, both Claude's maternal grandfather and uncle were ministers. Although his father was the minister, Claude's mother was much stricter in her religious practices, refusing even to go to the theatre.

The nine de Mestral children were a joyful bunch of six boys and three girls, Claude being sixth. The Christian faith, of course, ran deeply through their family life. Claude remembers hearing how his maternal grandfather, riding on a horse, rescued William Booth and his wife, founders of the Salvation Army. The Booths were about to be molested by a mob in Neuchâtel and his grandfather brought them to the safety of his house where they all hunkered down as the crowd hurled rocks at the windows. One of Claude's sisters eventually joined a Protestant religious order.

Life was happy for the de Mestral family in Lausanne. Then, in 1921, Claude's father died and they all discovered to their dismay that their parents' fortune had disappeared. It consisted mainly of shares in foreign firms like the tramways of Budapest, which were virtually worthless after the First World War. Although Claude had nearly finished his university studies, a family council decided that he should start an apprenticeship at a major food store in Lausanne to help pay the bills. For two-and-a-half years he earned money and learned the tricks of the trade. Then, with 200 francs in hand, he took the Orient Express to Paris in September, 1923.

Was he trying to escape family and traditions? Was he imitating his older brothers who had left for South America? In the roaring 20s, was the young man lured by the magic of Paris? By his own admission, he was drawn to the unknown and the chance to seek his own fortune.

This was the start of what Claude calls his "business period". What could be more natural for a Swiss than to work in the chocolate business? Through his mother, he was related to the Suchard family and, with the help of a cousin, Claude started working at their chocolate factory the day after he arrived in the French capital. Although by day he worked at the factory, at night he visited the museums, took night courses in history and arts at the Louvre and attended concerts. Cousins and acquaintances, including minister friends of his father, kept him company in the big city. Slowly, Claude realized that Switzerland, even with its strong international flavour, wasn't the centre of the earth.

After 15 months in Paris, Claude had an offer to work for an import company in India. Jumping at the chance, he left for the sub-continent, effectively ending the religious control of his family, which had carried over to his time in Paris.

The boat trip from Marseilles to Bombay through the Suez Canal was two weeks of marvellous discoveries. At work in Bombay, he had to learn English and Hindustani, the local language. Even more important, he had to learn the intricacies of the English colony. This led to a disquieting meeting with Mahatma Gandhi who asked him point-blank, "Young man, why have you come to my country? To help us or to make money?"

But, religion and social ferment weren't at the top of Claude's agenda at the time. He was living as "a joyous pagan" and, more than once, he says, he must have astonished the Indians with his lack of religious feeling.

Claude definitely didn't make his fortune in India. The import company was sold to a rich Bombay merchant and, sick with malaria, he had to take the the boat back to France and the Suchard factory in Paris. This time, he seriously set about learning the trade of chocolate maker, going from department to department in the factory. The plan was for the adventurous de Mestral to go to the United States where his cousins wanted to open up a Suchard branch. Finally, in October, 1927, Claude arrived in New York and started importing chocolate while his cousins were negotiating a merger with an American company. Claude De Mestral was well on his way to becoming a successful businessman. Eventually, he decided to leave the Wilbur-Suchard concern to join Nabisco, which had just bought Christie Brown Biscuits in Canada. Asked by the management if he'd like to go north to work at the new aquisition, he gladly accepted.

In September, 1929, Claude arrived in Quebec. He took the train to Montreal where he paid a visit to an old Swiss friend of his father. Professor Charles Bieler was minister of the French Protestant Bethany Church in Verdun, a Montreal suburb. The next day, he met his new boss at Christie Brown Biscuits in Toronto and discoved that his salary was less than half what he had earned in the United States. But, it was too late to turn back.

Mr. Bieler gave Claude a letter of introduction to one of his friends, Dr. Richard Roberts, minister at Toronto's Sherbourne United Church. One Sunday morning, without great enthusiasm, he went to the church, marvelling at the fact that he knew the hymns and appreciated the preaching. The next Sunday, Claude came back and gave the introductory letter to Dr. Roberts who promptly invited him home to lunch.

He still doesn't know exactly why he kept coming back to Sherbourne United. But, slowly, over time, his involvement helped him understand and make sense of the values cherished by his parents. He began to see their importance for everyone, including himself. "I then passed through a religious crisis— others would say a reconversion— and, in the spring of 1930, I became a member of that congregation," says Claude. More and more he was interested in what was happening at the church, particularly the discussions in the youth group. Meanwhile, he continued to make chocolate cookies at Christie's.

One day, as he was taking a walk, he thought he heard a small voice telling him he should become a minister. "Ridiculous!" he said out loud, given all the possibilities and money open to him in business. But, the question of ministry stayed there and kept haunting him. He decided to talk it over with Dr. Roberts who told him, "We cannot resolve this problem, Claude. We are simply going to pray to God and hand Him over the question, and you forget about it. One day, you will know what to do."

The advice made sense to Claude and he returned home greatly relieved. One month, two months, three months went by. Then, one morning, he simply woke up with the conviction that he should accept the call to ordained ministry. His life was set to take a new direction.

One of Claude's favourite Bible narratives is the story of Jonah and, through the years, he has emphasized different aspects of this small, Old Testament book. It's easy to laugh at the story of Jonah, supposedly eaten by a big fish and carried off kicking a screaming to do God's will. But, Claude de Mestral knows its deeper meaning very well. He left Switzerland and his Protestant family, forgetting all about God and religion. He went all the way to India and far-away Canada following a promising business career. But, in the end, like Jonah, he couldn't escape God's call to preach the Word.

Since the new convert didn't complete his studies due to his father's death, he entered a program to both finish his bachelor of arts and, at the same time, do his first year in theology at Toronto's Emmanuel College. It wasn't an easy time for Claude, working for two degrees while trying to live off a bursary and the extra money he made doing translations for Ontario Hydro.

The times were tough, but they were also very stimulating. Claude came back to school in the middle of the Great Depression at a time when his university professors were taking an active role in trying to help the needy. The acts and teachings of people like Dr. Line, a professor from England, Professor Lasserre from Switzerland and J. S. Woodsworth, founder of the Cooperative Commonwealth Federation (forerunner of the NDP), left a lasting impression on the theology student.

After his second year at Emmanuel, Claude decided to stop awhile to both practice what he was learning and make enough money to carry him through the rest of his studies.

For 18 months, Claude served the United Church in Bengough, Saskatchewan, a small village 150 kilometres south of Regina, as student minister. Bengough was the district centre for about 500 farms which were being hard-hit by the Depression and years of drought. In summertime, the wind would carry thick clouds of dust across the sky. In winter, heavy snowstorms would close all the roads.

Like many a student minister full of zeal, Claude set off to work hard. When he left, he had nine preaching posts, including an evening service in Bengough. He met French Protestants, isolated on the sparsely-populated prairies and, for the first time in his life, he conducted a service entirely in French. From time to time, he would even preach at the Lutheran Church, borrowing one of their liturgy books.

Even if distances are great in the west, the spiritual and social needs are the same as everywhere else in the country. At Christmastime, when the Anglican priest couldn't be present for the Christmas service, people turned to Claude and the United Church, asking for a shared service. A shared service wasn't so much the problem as the ability to provide Holy Communion. The student minister checked with his church elders, who agreed to prepare the Christmas service with Holy Communion. It was, without question, a little irregular for a student to give the sacrament with the help of a United Church elder and an Anglican church-warden, particularly when there was no official authorization. Just the same, the church was packed and the heartfelt singing told everyone it was all right. When his supervisor heard about the incident, he was relieved Claude hadn't asked for official advice, which would probably have come out against the idea.

Back studying in Toronto at the end of September, 1936, Claude met Lulu Bates. Lulu was the sister of his classmates and friends, John and Bob Bates and daughter of Dr. C.J. Bates, a missionary in Japan, where Lulu was born. It was love at first sight and it lasted for 40 years. Claude, having nothing more to offer than a minister's salary, wrote to Dr. Bates, then president of Kwansei Gakuin University in Kobe, Japan, asking him for his daughter's hand. The answer, which didn't take long to come back, was a resounding "go ahead."

Love and studies can go together, because Claude graduated with a string of A's in May, 1936 and was ordained. He and Lulu promptly married in June and went to Foloyet in northern Ontario for his ordinand charge. An important footnote to Claude's ordination was the fact that he finally felt reconciled with his mother, still living in Switzerland, now that he had become a minister like his father.

Claude and Lulu were scarcely installed in the small town of Foloyet when Claude received a long letter from professor Bieler telling him that Bethany was without a minister and, since he was French-speaking, it would be natural for him to come and serve the people in French.

The choice for Montreal was not a hard one for the young couple to make. Their departure for the big city proved to be much more than simply changing congregations. Little did Claude and Lulu realize when they arrived at Bonaventure Station in Montreal that they would spend 14 years in Verdun and see the birth of their four children there. They were also entering French Canada and Quebec, which many in English Canada liked to call "the priest-ridden province."

At that time, the United Church had difficulty grasping francophone needs and aspirations. The service to install the new French minister of this French parish was conducted solely in English (except for the hymns) by Montreal Presbytery. Claude de Mestral and Lulu couldn't help but feel the "two solitudes" living side by side, unable to meet each other. Francophones were a minority on an English continent, but French Protestants in Quebec were a still greater minority in a Catholic environment. Gradually, Claude and Lulu started to meet his parishioners and get acquainted with a wider circle of people in bustling Montreal.

Claude de Mestral's idea of a minister is someone who reaches out to meet people and brings the message to them. During a difficult strike in the textile industry at Valleyfield, south of Montreal, families of the strikers, mostly Catholics, asked Claude to come and speak to them. He asked them why they thought a Protestant minister should take a stand on the picket line. The strikers told him that their Catholic bishop received a gift from the company just before the strike started and they felt abandoned by the church. Not listening to the contrary advice of his fellow ministers, Claude accepted the invitation to show that the church was still on the strikers' side. Later, he went to speak to workers at Lachute, in the middle of another strike, and the young French minister was, by all reports, the most popular speaker of the evening.

The province of Quebec, at the time, was in the firm grip of Maurice Duplessis (premier from 1936-39 and 1944-59). Duplessis, among other things, started a form of private war against the Jehovah's Witnesses. His excesses prompted distinguished citizens, Protestant and Catholic, French and English, to join together and set up the first association for the defense of civil liberties. Among the founders were Claude de Mestral, Thérèse Casgrain, Roger Ouimet, Jacques Perreault and Frank Scott, a teacher at McGill University, who brought the Jehovah's Witnesses case all the way to the Supreme Court of Canada, finally winning years later.

His social involvement also helped make Claude a key journalistic witness to the mounting pressure for change both in Quebec and around the world. From 1940 to 1952, the United Church *Observer* published several articles by this French minister explaining the situation in Quebec. At the same time, Claude was editor of *L'Aurore*, the French monthly of Quebec's Protestant churches. In 1948, he went as a press correspondent to the founding meeting of the World Council of Churches in Amsterdam and sent back a number of articles to the Montreal *Daily Star* and *Saturday Night* magazine in Toronto. In other articles, written for Catholic readers, he tried to present what was behind the collective name of "Protestant".

It all seems so logical now but, back then, Claude kept thinking he was overreaching himself. In 1952, he was asked to become secretary of the International Committee of Christian Literature for Africa. At first, he felt he should refuse, but the sense of adventure was still very much a part of Claude and his family. Not really knowing what he was getting into, he took his family and all their furniture and they set off for the Committee's headquarters in London. What followed were seven years filled with rich experiences, among them three long trips to the Portuguese, French and English colonies of Africa.

Holding the unique position of a bilingual minister from Canada, without a colonial past, Claude was equally at ease in the French and English parts of Africa and he won a good measure of acceptance from the Africans. Much of his work involved locating Africans who could write well and write on Christian subjects— not so much for the masses but, first, for the Christian workers.

The simple logistical problems were as huge as the African continent itself. The Committee published two magazines, a monthly entitled *Listen*, featuring Christian material, and a tri-monthly called *Books for Africa*, with a circulation of 5,000 and sections in English, French and Portuguese. Claude had to find writers, publishers, printers and financing for books destined primarily for Africans. The abundant racism of the time didn't make his work any easier. Everywhere, the churches were in the hands of white people who had a hard time giving real responsibilities to blacks.

Claude is particularly proud of having been the last Committee secretary based in London. Due to Claude and many others, the Committee headquarters was divided and transferred to Nairobi, Kenya, Kitwe, Northern Rhodesia (now Zambia) and Yaoundé, Cameroun. All this happened before the great decolonization movement of the 1960s.

During his last trip to Africa, Claude had his most startling encounter. The year before, he had read a very good article by a Muslim writer entitled, "The Convergence of Religions". Knowing he would visit Bamako in Mali on his last voyage, Claude de Mestral wrote to this Muslim asking to meet him. The Muslim came to the airport and, placing his two hands on Claude's shoulders, he said, "My brother in God, I salute you" and he kissed Claude on both cheeks. Here was a Muslim greeting a Christian and ready to talk about common problems concerning religions and the lack of faith in young people. Before leaving Africa, Claude discovered that "the brothers and sisters" also included Muslim brothers and sisters.

Coming back to Canada after seven years with the literature committee, Claude could find neither a French ministry nor a post within Montreal Presbytery. Finally, with the help of an old friend from Emmanuel College, he got a posting to the United Church at Noranda-Rouyn, a mining centre in northwestern Quebec. To his surprise, he found out that he had a number of engineers, chemists, geologists, doctors and professors among his parishioners. Preaching to such audiences required a little extra preparation. It also brought him face to face with some old realities. With English-speaking people in positions of command and French-speaking people as the workers, Quebec's social and political questions began to catch up with Claude once again. Patiently, he tried to bring francophones and anglophones, Catholics and Protestants together by creating discussion groups.

Then, circumstances gave the whole population a chance to work at a rapprochement. North of Noranda, a new mining centre was opening up at Matagami and already workers were being transferred to the new site. Tradition and law required that two schools be built, one French and Catholic and the other English and Protestant. But, these practical people decided otherwise and only one school was built— a bilingual school— which left the religious teachings to the clergy.

As for the church, the spirit of Vatican II was having its effect even in these remote places. The Catholic bishop quickly agreed to a common building which would house the Catholic, United and Anglican churches. Construction of the new, L-shaped church was completed immediately after the instant town's hospital. On church dedication day, Claude de Mestral said a prayer of blessing for the Catholic altar. Things do change— even among the churches.

During this very busy period of his life, Claude was instrumental in founding a new university at Sudbury. Laurentian University was formed through an amalgamation of colleges supported by the Anglican, Catholic and United churches. It was greatly helped along the way by the moral support and financial gifts of northern parishes such as Claude's. Once opened, he contributed to the university's academic life by preparing various conferences on Africa.

Before long, the whole de Mestral family got into the university business. One by one, Claude's and Lulu's boys were leaving home to pursue their education in Boston, Toronto and Kingston. The last of their children followed her parents back to Montreal and enrolled at McGill University.

After his stint at Noranda-Rouyn, Claude returned to

Montreal, but in a new and entirely different pastoral post. Concerned by the increasing number of persons not going to any church service, the United Church decided to set up a project aimed at reaching out to these people. Never one to refuse a challenge, Claude de Mestral threw himself into this Montreal Presbytery experiment.

A nine-member committee (five lay persons and four ministers) guided Claude as he put together the pieces to create a completely new centre, a community meeting place. Open to everyone, the centre was set up with books and magazines, a movie room and an office. It was situated downtown, right next to Sir George Williams University. Bilingual, ecumenical, open to believers and non- believers, the centre wanted to be present for people beyond the church buildings.

The concept was accepted easily, but it took six months for Claude to have the name "Dialogue", reflecting both the program's bilingual character and its openness, approved. Members of the founding committee were reluctant to have a church centre with no mention of the United Church.

But, finally, the word "Dialogue" stuck and the new centre worked hard to live up to its name. When the nearby university students revolted against what they felt was an impersonal administration and started throwing computer files out the windows, Claude de Mestral told his secretary, "Don't stop making coffee!" Dialogue's door was thrown open to protesting students and they were surprised to find a movie playing which showed the conflicts between people and machines. All day, students and teachers kept coming in. The movie was shown time and again, while various ministers explained how Christians were concerned with these questions. From then on, Dialogue had its own special place in the city.

Not having a traditional parish, Claude de Mestral didn't have to retire at age 65 like other ministers. He was able to pursue his mission at Dialogue for five more years. At the same time, he was getting more and more involved in political activities. He was part of a group demanding lower bus fares for senior citizens. Family planning has also been an important issue on Claude's agenda. He even contested, and lost, a race for a position on the Protestant School Board of Greater Montreal.

Leaving Dialogue in June 1973, after eight years of

service, Claude told the press that Christians should develop wider social concerns than the financial struggles of their own congregations. It's not the building that's important, he noted and, in a big city like Montreal, many churches could be torn down. In their places, apartment buildings for seniors and the needy could be built, with a room reserved for worship. Claude is still amazed that some churches don't get more involved with the people right in their own neighbourhoods.

For Claude de Mestral, retirement meant having more free time to work on social and political causes. Practising what he preaches— "Every Christian should be engaged in work for a political party"— he was one of the founding members of the Montreal Citizens' Movement in 1974. His fight for lower bus fares had gotten Claude involved in city politics.

He also caught the attention of the New Democratic Party. In three consecutive federal elections in the riding of Westmount (1970, 1979 and 1980) he gallantly upheld the party's colours, gaining votes every time. To emphasize the energy crisis, he campaigned in a horse-drawn carriage.

Claude's election losses meant nothing when compared to another very personal loss during the same period. On a summer morning, Lulu, his companion of 40 years, quietly passed away. The sadness of parting was tempered by the memories of a very special relationship.

Today, Claude de Mestral continues to live life with vigour. You can still meet him in Montreal, actively participating in meetings of the new, French-language Laurentian Presbytery or having political meetings in his dining room. When seniors, furious at the federal government's plan to de-index old age pensions, converged on Ottawa for a mass demonstration two years ago, their eloquent spokesperson was none other than Claude de Mestral.

Claude is currently working on his memoirs, which he has dedicated to his grandchildren. Very appropriately, they open with this thought out of *Winnie the Pooh* : "I wonder what exciting is going to happen today?"

MARION KIRKWOOD:
COMPANION ON THE WAY

by Gary Kenny

There are many discoveries you can make about people by letting your eyes wander around their living quarters. On Marion Kirkwood's mantle sits an ebony carving, the handiwork of the Makonde tribe of southern Tanzania. Over the mantle hangs a hand-woven tapestry depicting an African village scene and tucked into a corner beside an armchair is an African drum, decorated with a geometric pattern and covered with a canvas-coloured animal skin stretched taut. These and other cultural artifacts on display confirm that the people living here have a strong affection for things African. In fact, that may be something of an understatement. For 11 years the Kirkwood's, Marion and Jim, were United Church missionaries in the southern African country of Zambia. Today, Jim Kirkwood is an area secretary for Africa within the national Division of World Outreach.

Looking over these artifacts of a different culture, you begin to realize that here is a woman who spent a significant portion of her life immersed in the life of an African nation, a developing nation with much poverty and none of the rampant consumerism of Canadian society. Here is a woman who returned home 12 years ago and was forced to readapt to a country that is both wealthy and wasteful of its resources.

Marion Kirkwood is known throughout the United Church for her contribution to the church's mission. She has served the church both overseas and in Canada. For the past four years she has chaired the national Division of World Outreach's Animation Committee and she's an active, long-standing member of Trinity-St. Paul's United Church in Toronto. But, even though Marion has made all these mission contributions, surprisingly enough the word "mission" causes her to wince. The word makes her uncomfortable, she says. "I almost decided against (being interviewed for this book) because of the unpleasant images the word 'mission' conjures up for me and, I think, for most people. At one point in my life I was probably very comfortable with the images that the word brought to mind — outreach, going somewhere far away, telling the good news, development — images that come to most people's minds when they hear or think of the word. But, I no longer am."

Marion's discomfort arises from the fact that for centuries, and to some extent still today, the word "mission" has been tied to patriarchal images and structures. Marion tells a story to illustrate. She talks about growing up in small-town, southwestern Ontario, the daughter of a United Church minister. Returned missionaries would sometimes come to my father's church, she says. They'd talk about their experiences spreading the gospel in exotic, foreign lands among strange and unfamiliar cultures. They were always full of stories about how their subjects had divested themselves of their pagan, animist beliefs and had embraced Jesus Christ as their saviour. Sometimes, she adds, the missionaries even brought photographic slides with them to illustrate their work in living colour. Marion says she never doubted the missionaries' enthusiasm for doing the "work of the Lord" or their undeniable good intentions of helping people. But, she says, "I was always left with the image of the 'great white father' going out and spreading the good news, evangelizing the people. That was my perception of mission as a child." She adds that the church is still founded largely on patriarchal structures and, for that reason, she has a problem with the church's mission today.

Born a child of the manse during the Depression years (1933) in small-town Ontario, Marion Woods grew up on mission, ministry and moving. Her father, a United Church minister, moved the family around to small Ontario towns like Sparta, Exeter and Thedford. Marion later attended Victoria College at the University of Toronto and the United Church Training School (now the Centre for Christian Studies). In July, 1957, she married the young ordinand, Jim Kirkwood, went west and started a new phase of her life in yet another manse.

However, Marion's adult environment wasn't destined to be the same one in which she grew up. In 1962, the Kirkwoods made a radical departure. They applied and became missionaries of The United Church of Canada and received a placement in Northern Rhodesia (now Zambia). According to Marion, the 11 years she and Jim subscquently spent in Zambia actually comprised three separate terms: 1962-1966, 1967-71 and 1973-1976. In between, there were two furloughs back in Canada.

Our first missionary posting, says Marion, was in the rural village of Kalulwa. It was a town that would probably be considered remote in Canadian terms. The nearest city was many milcs away and there were no telephones. The only means of communication was a single, two-way radio which was used once a day to make contact with a mission hospital 100 kilometres down the valley. Jim had been assigned a parish with about 20 points and to serve those congregations he had to leave on a Wednesday morning and he wouldn't return until the following Sunday night. "I was basically alone for three weeks out of four," she says, "with three small children, one a three month old baby."

As memories of that time begin to flood back, Marion acknowledges that the experience had quite an impact on her. "It helped me develop a lot of self-reliance as a woman," she says. "You had to learn self-reliance in a situation like that, where your partner is away so much of the time. When I got over the initial shock of being left alone with small children in a strange culture, I began to develop an ability to cope. I discovered I could manage quite well (as a part-time single) parent and knowing that gave me a lot of confidence in myself and in my abilities to solve problems on my own." Those first few years in Zambia taught me things about myself that still help me today, she adds. "When Jim goes away to Africa for three months now and the freezer breaks down, I don't have to depend on a father or a husband to solve the problem. I can take care of things myself."

If that first term in Zambia was a formative one, the second was even more so. In fact, it would leave such an indelible mark on Marion that even today the memory of those days remains sensitive to the touch. As she begins to tell another story her voice grows quiet. She chooses her words very carefully, not because she's worried about divulging private information, but because after 15 years the emotions tied up in the experience are still close to the surface.

Pregnant with her fourth child, she'd gone to the city of Kitwe, in the southern part of Zambia to meet Jim, who'd been away for several days. It was there in Kitwe that son Timothy James was born. But, two weeks after the birth, the very morning on which they'd planned to return to their second-term mission post at Kalulushi with their newborn son, they awoke to find that Timothy James had died in his sleep. The cause of death was Sudden Infant Death Syndrome— "crib-death" as it's more commonly known— a form of death which baffles medical experts even today.

Timothy's death was devastating. We were thousands of miles from our families, Marion says, and forced to deal with a tragedy like that. During that painful time, the Kirkwoods did learn, however, that while they may have been an ocean away from their family, by no means were they alone. The outpouring of emotional support from their Zambian friends was overwhelming. Marion explains that, in Zambia, when someone dies, friends, neighbours and relatives will come and stay with the bereaved family for days on end. They'll stick with the family day and night, virtually never leaving their side. They come to help out and just to offer their love and support. In the Kirkwood's case, however, Marion thinks it was out of respect for differences in culture and custom that their Zambian friends and acquaintances came and stayed only during the day and left she and Jim and the children to themselves at night. So strong was the moral support from Zambian friends that even people who didn't hear about the death until three and four months later still came to see the Kirkwoods— some travelling considerable distances.

As Marion reaches further back into the memories of that time and reflects on the gift of love and support given by those people, tears fill her eyes, disclosing the fact that some wounds never completely heal. "You put these kinds of experiences away in the back of your mind, but they still come out," she says, her voice breaking. And, then, she offers a very human response to a very painful experience. "It perhaps sounds callous but, even if Timothy had died at five years of age, we would have had five years worth of memories to cherish. But, two weeks — so little time for a life to be lived, so much potential lost, so much joy never to be known." If it hadn't been for her Zambian family, Marion says, she doesn't know how she would have coped. The support of those people "really showed me what the community of believers could be and, because of that, the experience was a healing one."

A child of the manse, a minister's wife, a missionary, a woman touched by both joy and tragedy, Marion Kirkwood has moved through many transitions so far in her life. She likes to tell the story of how she and her sister had sworn as children that they'd never marry ministers. Tears turn to laughter as she begins. When my sister and I were teenagers we vowed that never, under any circumstances, would we marry ministers. As daughters of an itinerant preacher in the United Church, she explains, we knew well what married life with a minister could be like: husband never home on Sundays, away for hours each week on pastoral calls and, of course, the endless committee meetings. It seemed as if Dad had never been home. But, in the end, neither sister could keep her oath. Whether it was a strange quirk of divine providence or some predilection they were born with, both sisters ended up walking down the aisle with men of the cloth.

I began married life almost literally married to the church, says Marion. Like my mother before me, I assumed the role of "a typical minister's wife." When Jim was assigned a pastorate in rural Saskatchewan after we were married, I dutifully followed and I dutifully did all the things expected of a woman of my station in life: I taught Sunday School, directed the junior choir, devoted much of my time to volunteer activities in the community, raised a family and taught piano from the manse, where I could keep an eye on the children.

Before marrying Jim, Marion had been a student at the University of Toronto's Victoria College and had studied for two years at the United Church Training School (now called the Centre for Christian Studies). However, getting married seemed to extinguish any aspirations she might have had of pursuing a career in the ordained ministry herself. "I got married and became an unpaid assistant to the minister," she laughs, "a helpmate."

From the point of view of being a minister's wife, Marion says that the Kirkwood's first two stints in Zambia were in many ways a repeat performance of life in the Canadian west. Once again, she involved herself in volunteer work in the community and the church. The only difference was that now she was playing the role in a different country, a different continent and a different culture. In some ways, it must have seemed like life with Dad all over again. However, now there were three young children in the picture and, instead of a few hours here and there, Jim was away for days at a time serving his 20 point parish.

With young family in tow, Marion and Jim returned to Canada in 1971 for a year's furlough. Marion recalls arriving back in her native land with a feeling of dissatisfaction. She yearned to escape her typecasting as a minister's wife and to "pursue something for myself." But, what that "something" was eluded her for some time.

One day, while driving with Jim in their Volkswagen mini-bus somewhere in northwest Toronto, "it just came to me." All of a sudden, she says, "I turned to Jim and said, 'I know what I want to do. I want to teach music to handicapped kids.'" The realization "just came out of the blue," she adds. When I started to reflect on just what might have influenced my decision, a chain of influential experiences suddenly became obvious. I had always been musical, having learned to play the piano at an early age. In Zambia, I discovered that I really liked teaching children. And, from the experience of raising Paul, our eldest son, who was born mentally handicapped, I had learned about the many special gifts handicapped people have to offer so-called "normal" society. Finally, living in an isolated sector of rural Zambia had tough-ened my resolve to make it on my own. "With Jim being away so much and with three small children to look after, I had to develop a lot of self-reliance," she says. "In that single moment, driving along with Jim, all of those experiences just came together. It was one of life's little miracles."

As a result of that one revelation, Marion decided to attend teachers' college. For the first time in her higher education life she enrolled in a secular school. "I'd had enough of the church context for a while," she says. It meant that the family would have to apply to the national church to stay in Canada a second consecutive year before returning to Zambia. So Jim applied for and was granted a year's leave of absence.

Recalls Marion, "Those two years weren't easy." They were a challenging and sometimes difficult time involving struggle and conflict with myself and with Jim. "I was expanding my understanding of what being a woman, mother and partner in marriage might mean."

Suddenly, Marion and Jim had a number of things to re-think and work through. They had to learn new patterns of relationship, how to work conflicts through, how to better share parenting roles and how to work closer together on household matters. "In those two years I went a long way toward establish-ing a new identity as a woman," says Marion. Perhaps most important, she adds, "I had to work through with Jim just what was wrong with the life I had lived up until then and why I suddenly wanted to change things."

Those days weren't easy for Jim, says Marion. However, "he was and still is very understanding. I consider myself very fortunate indeed to have a partner like Jim with whom I have been able to work things through. I know many women my age whose marriages either have or are breaking up, and very often it's over this kind of issue. They want more for themselves, their own identity as women, but they have partners who lack sensi-tivity to and understanding of what a woman's life has been."

That second year in Canada also proved to be a very formative one for Jim. A course with Canadian Urban Training (CUT) had a major impact on his own views of mission work in the church. CUT's justice-oriented approach to urban ministry inspired him to rethink his views on ministry and mission in a Third World context. Like Marion, he would return to Zambia having undergone a kind of personal transformation. Based on a deeper commitment to working in solidarity with poor and oppressed people, his ministry would become much more politi-cized and the changed nature of his relationship with Marion had broadened his sense of partnership.

With Marion graduated from teachers' college and Jim from CUT, the Kirkwood family once again packed their bags and climbed aboard a plane bound for Zambia. Their posting this time was in Lusaka, Zambia's capital city. Jim resumed his duties as a minister and Marion took a position teaching English immersion to grade one students. She decided not to involve herself in Jim's ministry at all. "I felt I had to withdraw myself physically (from his ministry)," she explains. "I officially stopped being a minister's wife. I didn't pull out of church life altogether, but I pretty much did my own thing."

Marion's partial withdrawal from church life caused

some uneasiness among women in the parish. Although she hadn't known them before, they seemed to know all about her and about the kind of life she led during her two previous terms in Zambia. They couldn't understand the reasons for the change. "I avoided trying to explain to them the real reasons," Marion admits. She opted, instead, to say that teaching left her no time for other kinds of activities. "It was actually true," she points out, "but most of the women didn't understand that. Most of them were active in church life as well as being employed full-time."

The Kirkwoods moved back to Canada to stay in 1976 and Jim became the Division of World Outreach's Africa Secretary. His three terms in Zambia, his CUT training and, perhaps, even the changes in marital relationship brought about by Marion, had made Jim much more aware of the politics of injustice.

Marion notes that Jim's commitment to justice influenced her to the extent that her role as wife, mother and woman also took on a political dimension. She developed an integrated (some might say radical) view of why the lives of so many people in the world are bereft of justice. "I saw very clearly the links between such 'isms' as sexism, racism, capitalism — and even handicapism," she says. "They have a common root cause and that cause is power" — people wanting power and willing to do just about anything to get it, people with power who are trying desperately to hold on to it and everywhere people who horde power and selfishly refuse to share it.

"Handicapism" is one "ism" that Marion has done considerable battle with. Bringing up son Paul who, because of a lack of oxygen during birth, is mentally handicapped, has given her first-hand knowledge of how society discriminates against those whom it conveniently labels "sub-normal".

A handicapped person challenges some of the values of Western society and culture, Marion says. There's a hierarchy based on intelligence, intellect, education and competence. People with mental handicaps, because they're judged to be unintelligent, hard to educate and generally incompetent, are pushed to the bottom. But intelligence, or what society defines as intelligence, is only one aspect of our total humanity. "It's a very important (aspect) but others may be as much if not more important." Take the ability of the handicapped person to love. "Even though it may sound very stereotypical to say so, my experience is that most of the handicapped people I know have a great capacity to love...it's difficult to put into words. There's just something so basic, something that touches another person's personhood and illuminates something good about themselves that they perhaps didn't know before."

She says that music has played an important role in helping her to communicate with Paul. Handicapped people are generally "very responsive to music," she adds. "Sometimes it's the rhythm, sometimes the sound." Learning to communicate with Paul using music as an aid has taught Marion that you can communicate with people in other ways besides talking. You don't always have to have an intellectual conversation, she says. Sometimes all that's needed is to share a little music, a little art and some quiet time.

However, adds Marion, such little miracles or revelations only come to those with patience — those who are prepared to listen and wait and be open to the possibility of something deeper. Most people, she says, especially when they encounter a handicapped person whose appearance they find physically grotesque or strange, totally dismiss that person as a human being. That person is a "retard" or whatever demeaning label one wants to apply. On the other hand, "you can try just to be with that person. Suddenly you sense communication when, before, the wisdom of the day was telling you that no communication was possible." It's during moments like that, she says, when the "impossible" — the little miracles — are most likely to happen.

Life in Zambia has left its mark on the Kirkwoods in many different ways. Lifestyle is one example. In Zambia, the Kirkwoods learned to live very modestly, like the local inhabitants. There were none of the "embellishments" of Canadian consumer society and there was none of the waste. The frantic pace of North American life was far, far away.

When we returned to Canada, says Marion, we brought back a simpler set of values than what we'd left with. We wanted to carry back to Canada the lifestyle we'd learned living among our Zambian brothers and sisters. "We've been back for more than 11 years now. Some of those customs we've continued, some we've not."

The Kirkwoods made an intentional decision as a family to do without a car, which they did for eight years. But, eventually, Marion took her present job as a consultant with the Metro Toronto School Board, helping teachers plan special education programs for young people in the 14 to 21 age group. With the new job, a car became essential. "Now," says Marion with a laugh, "I can't do without it."

The Kirkwoods also tried to become less dependent on the food marketing and processing system. They began growing some of their own food and searching out alternative food sources for things they couldn't grow themselves. They even joined a food co-op. "We know we haven't had much of an impact on North American consumer culture," Marion admits, "but it somehow helps to know that you have at least some measure of control over something as important as what you eat."

The Kirkwoods, especially Jim, also returned to Canada with a commitment to co-operative living. We would have preferred to find co-operative housing, says Marion, but, with four children, three of them teenagers, it was almost impossible to find four-bedroom, co-op housing quickly. They ended up buying their present home in Toronto's Riverdale district. Although the Kirkwoods didn't achieve their co-operative housing ideal, they have established their own version. Now that the oldest three children have moved away from home, there's more room for the "people in transit" who always find their way to the Kirkwood's door. As Marion was speaking, her house was also home for a black South African couple exiled from their country for their political activities against apartheid. "It's not a true co-operative living arrangement because we own the house," she says. "But, we do try to live co-operatively in terms of doing housework, making meals, shopping for food — everyone contributes to the life of the household and we seem able to work things out as a group."

Marion Kirkwood's life experiences give her a tremendous insight into the mission of the church. Although the word "mission" still conjures up some patriarchal, "holier than thou" images for her because of her childhood, she also cares very deeply that "mission" should come to mean newer, richer and healthier things to her church.

She talks about China missionary Katherine Hockin as a way of illustrating the gap between the mission of her childhood and the mission of today. Katherine was born in China to missionary parents and served there herself for many years as a missionary of the United Church. Her own inner struggle with the meaning of the church's mission had a great influence on Marion.

After the communists came to power in 1949, everything about the West, including its missionaries, fell out of favour with the Chinese. As one of those missionaries, Katherine was asked by the church in China to leave the country. Here was a person who had served the Chinese church faithfully for years. Now, she was being told that her services were no longer required. For the Chinese church, it was a growing-up period, Marion says, and time to cut free from Western "parent" churches. For Katherine, it was a time of mixed blessings. While she was happy about the emergence of a strong, independent church in China, she couldn't hide the pain of separation from the Chinese people she loved so much. The complete experience gave rise to much reflection about the role of Western "parent" churches in the Third World, particulary as the new national churches rightfully asserted their independence.

Back in Canada, says Marion, "Katherine was still processing her experience and telling her story and beginning to look at the mission of the church in an analytical way. As I listened to Katherine, I stopped just accepting all the wonderful stories of mission. Through her own critical experience, I was able to develop my own critique of the church's mission."

Is the mission of the church finally on the right track now? "It would be presumptuous of me to say whether the church's mission is right," says Marion. "The church is doing so many different things in different places. In some places it is being faithful, in others it isn't. To say what is right or wrong about the church's mission would be making a value judgement I have no right to make."

While not wanting to make value judgements on mission, Marion does feel there are some important guidelines for faithful mission. The church is fulfilling its gospel mandate most "where it is acting in solidarity with people who are oppressed," she says. "Where we are seeking to liberate each other, then we're being at least a little bit faithful to what God is about in the world." Where we are continuing to hang on to (irrelevant) traditions and structures, then we're not being faithful. She's quick to add, "I would never presume to say to those people, 'You are wrong.'" We must keep the dialogue going. We must "see both sides (of issues) and yet still remain true to what we believe ourselves."

Marion has a strong sense of what direction she'd like to see the church's mission take. We're currently in the partnership mode, she explains, the sense of which is supposed to be captured in the slogan "mutuality in mission". "But, I'm not sure we really understand what partnership means or what being true 'companions' means." She feels that the phrase "companions on the way", coined by Asian theologians, better captures the sense of mission that's reflected in the gospel.

For Marion, there's a definite distinction between "partnership" and "companionship". Partnership implies that we have to support others in their struggle to be liberated. But, in order to truly support and contribute to the liberation of another, we must at the same time be working to liberate ourselves. As we give to them, we must also receive from them. We must recognize the need to be liberated within ourselves and to receive from them. "That's not how mutuality in mission has been interpreted and understood," she says.

Marion feels that the church still takes too much of a "doing for" approach to mission. At some point during her life, she says, she discovered that mission wasn't a "doing for" as much as it was a "doing with" or, better yet, a "being with". "Being with," adds Marion, "is why companionship is so important and meaningful at this time in my life."

Marion struggles for a word that better captures her sense of the church's mission. "The closest I can come is 'journey'," she says. "As I look at my life — what I've done and seen, what I'm doing now and what I hope to do in the future — it seems like a journey, a journey with companions who share commitment to loving relationships, justice and recognition of and respect for the personhood that's within all people."

Companionship — "being with" people — has always been important to Marion. It's really a central thread which has run through the fabric of her entire life. Marion has "been with" people in some very special ways and under some very special circumstances. She's been with the loving people of Zambia who took time away from their own lives to be with Marion and Jim during a time of great loss. She's been with Paul, who she says has taught her so much about loving others. She's been with Jim, her partner in marriage for 30 years, who supported her need to achieve her own identity. She's been with close friends and colleagues in the "house church" with whom she and Jim meet and worship. And, she's been with the many people for whom the Kirkwood's rambling, five-bedroom house has been a home away from home on their own winding journeys through life. Each one of those precious experiences has its own specific meaning. Each evokes a different memory, some happy and some sad. Each is a miracle on Marion Kirkwood's unique mission journey.

In the future, Marion says she'd like to take some concentrated time to develop what she calls her "spiritual side". "I need to explore my own spirituality," she says. Marion makes it clear she's not talking about any pietistic notion of spirituality nor one that's divorced from action. In fact, she believes there's always an active component to spirituality. But, she also feels that the social action side of her life is full to overflowing while the spiritual side has been neglected.

In reality, so much of Marion's life, both in Canada and Africa has been imbued with a deep and motivating spirituality. The desire to "be with" people in a loving and faithful way is, without doubt, part of a spiritual journey. But, now, Marion wonders out loud if this isn't a good opportunity to set some time apart for herself— a creative or "re-creative" time to explore and fulfill some of her own personal aspirations.

In fact, Marion will be taking a leave of absence in 1989 and she hopes to explore some new career possibilities. She senses that her career journey will take a major turn in the next couple of years, perhaps into writing educational books or even some short stories. "I've always wanted to develop literacy materials for the handicapped," she says, returning to a familiar theme.

Marion shares one last thought about her own journey. The opportunities and experiences, happy or sad, that we encounter along the way, she notes, can either disempower us or we can take control of them and exercise our own influence. "Maybe that's my mission in life— to try to find the creative responses to what's happening around me, and not only to me, but to the world as well."

BRUCE MCLEOD:
LOVER OF GOD'S WORLD

by Noelle Boughton

The Very Rev. N. Bruce McLeod, a former United Church Moderator, believes no one can really see God by just sitting in a church. You have to go into the world and see people's lives and hurts to really experience God's spirit.

That's something Bruce, a southern Ontario United Church minister for 35 years, practices as well as he preaches. In fact, just days before he was interviewed for this book, the 58-year-old McLeod was in strife-torn Haiti, listening to rebel gunfire outside his hotel room door and fearing for his life.

That wasn't out of step for Bruce who has, for years, preached a message of Christian mission as the pursuit of justice. He has done that by stepping into the world outside the church as a political candidate, newspaper columnist and provincial human rights commission member. But, he has also done that by walking into some of the world's more dangerous and troubled corners. Slim, brown-eyed and quietly energetic, Bruce has strolled down Vietnamese streets during its war, worked in a Costa Rican project for abandoned children and visited Central American refugees in Honduran villages.

"I've really found it important down the years to seize every opportunity to get out into different parts of the world because I think it's very hard to be a church in a rich part of a hungry world," says Bruce.

"There's gospel backing for that, you know," he adds, mixing Bible passages with philosophy as deftly as others drop names. "Jesus says it's hard for a rich person to get into the kingdom of heaven, not because they're bad people but just because we're so surrounded with things that we don't see the world as it is."

"I grew up in this city. I love it," he says, as he waves his arm at a nearby window, behind which sprawls Toronto's grey buildings. "But I feel there are very narrow horizons here and there are walls around so it's like we're hermetically sealed off from the rest of the world. So I've always needed to get out of this rich part of the world. I believe you learn not just about God's world, but about God by going to some of these hurting places."

Most recently, Bruce learned of God's world in Haiti. In November, 1987, he had been out of his three-year post at Toronto's Metropolitan United Church for five months and was enjoying one of the "working sabbaticals" which have peppered his ministry when he was asked to go to Haiti. One of two United Church representatives on an international, inter-church observation team, he was to watch the first Haitian elections in 30 years — a major step for the small Caribbean nation which had deposed its dictator president, Jean-Claude "Baby Doc" Duvalier, 22 months earlier. Fearing Duvalier supporters might disrupt the election, Haiti's Independent Electoral Council — which organized the election — asked the Caribbean Council of Churches to appoint observers. "They believed the presence of the world's eyes through us would provide some security from people whom they thought would prefer not to have everybody know the awful things they were doing," Bruce says.

But, it didn't work. When Haiti's polls opened November 30, terrorist squads moved in with machine guns and knives. The Council closed the polls three hours after they opened, but not before 34 people were killed and 67 others wounded.

Most of the violence was in Haiti's capital of Port-au-Prince and Bruce was in Les Cayes, a city of 30,000 people located 150 kilometres west. There had been no shooting there for five months but, in the middle of the night before the election, Bruce heard shots "right outside our door." People were shot at during polling. Bruce's cab was followed and it raced down one-way streets to shake its pursuers. "I found myself thinking should I sit in the centre of the car (to avoid bullets) or should I get over to the side?" he says, admitting his sense of terror until the car finally veered off.

On his return trip to Port-au-Prince, Bruce was almost caught in a riot when his group stopped for news from a local pastor, whom an angry mob suspected of hiding ballots. Reporting in his bi-weekly Toronto *Star* column days later, he recalled his stomach-tightening terror as he stood beside the pastor, fearing "something uncontrollable seemed about to be unleashed." Finally, under an armed guard, he and the others made it safely away. Terror notwithstanding, Bruce says he never once wished he'd stayed away from Haiti. "I guess my sense is always that it's sort of a privilege to be there."

For Bruce, the privilege was being out in God's world, seeing God's spirit at work. "The biblical thrust that has always moved me is that God so loved the WORLD. It doesn't say God so loved the church or God so loved Canada. The church is loved, I think, only as it is available to the rush of God's love for the whole world, the whole earth, and certainly I think that our job is to be available to that Spirit. You meet that Spirit out in the rest of the world. I met it in Haiti with people in tough situations."

God's spirit, for Bruce McLeod, is embodied by the people in those tough and often dangerous places. "I had the sense, seeing people's faces in these areas, that they shine," he says. "It's as though, in the paining parts of the world, the crust is pulled back in a way that it isn't here, unless you go downtown (where the homeless, runaways and prostitutes live). It's as though there's some presence there." Quoting the Bible verse about the light shining in the darkness, he says that he sees this light "shining in people's faces, these faithful people who, in these tough situations, somehow are closer to the world-loving presence of God."

That is, says Bruce, why he treasures these experiences which would intimidate many others. "I grow through them. I grow through my knowledge of God," he says. "For me, these world experiences, all of them, are religious experiences."

Born in Toronto on February 5, 1929, Norman Bruce McLeod was raised in an upper middle class family where his mother, Maude, was a former social worker and his father, Norman, chaired the large, international Moore Corporation, which is a major producer of business forms. Bruce notes his family's simple roots — one grandfather was a lake sailor, the other a teacher. But, a generation later, the McLeods were wealthy enough for Bruce, one of three children, to attend high school at Toronto's prestigious Upper Canada College. He went on to get a Bachelor of Arts at the University of Toronto, Bachelor of Divinity at Toronto's Emmanuel College, Master of Arts at New York's Columbia University and a Doctor of Theology at New York's Union Theological Seminary.

He was ordained in the United Church in 1953 and says the move didn't surprise either of his Presbyterian-raised parents, who were already involved with the church. (His father chaired the United Church's Division of Finance for 20 years.) Bruce served a succession of southern Ontario churches, including Victoria Harbour, Westdale in Hamilton, Bloor Street and Metropolitan in downtown Toronto and Richmond Hill United. He and his first wife, Jewel, raised three daughters and Bruce began to travel as well as minister.

In 1966, he went to Japan and Taiwan to represent the United Church *Observer* on a three-week press trip. While there, he decided to go to Vietnam because it was so close. "It surprised me that nobody else wanted to go, so I went alone. I simply couldn't miss going." Seeing the results of that war was, for Bruce, a turning point. "I'd never heard gun-fire before and that war was where I first heard it," he recalls. "I also saw children falling asleep in the street at nights." Thinking of his daughters sleeping in their own beds and rooms, oblivious to this reality, he adds, "I remember wondering how I could help those little girls of mine grow up in the real world, to worry about the real things."

On his return home, Bruce's profile also began to rise as the secular press reported on his statements urging Canada's government to tax church properties. He hasn't pursued the issue in a decade, but he still believes in it. "The churches get a free ride in this country, so there tend to be too many church buildings." The churches struggle on, some with heavy mortgages, and refuse to close or amalgamate, so "taxation could be like the rod of the Assyrians coming to move God's people when they don't move by themselves." The only exemptions he'd urge is for churches which do something, such as a drop-in centre, to benefit the general community.

The taxation issue drew attention to Bruce in the late 1960s and early 1970s when he ran twice for the two-year position of United Church Moderator. In 1968, he was runner-up to Bob McClure but in 1972 he was elected and, at 43, became the United Church's youngest-ever Moderator and the first Moderator born in the United Church.

Looking back on his time as Moderator, Bruce prefaces his memories with a chuckle about being asked his official opinion on rising bread prices. "The trouble is, when you're Moderator," he says, "people ask you questions on all kinds of subjects and you begin to think your opinion is worth more than other people's." While in office, Bruce says proudly, he avoided being engulfed by the national church system by staying rooted in his local church, Bloor Street United. He enjoyed travelling across the country, meeting members of smaller communities and getting a "sense of the family of the United Church."

As Moderator, Bruce continued to urge inter-church, inter-faith and international co-operation. He was disappointed when the United, Anglican and Disciples of Christ churches failed to unite. But, he was pleased when the angry rift between the United Church and Canada's Jewish community over the United Church Observer's alleged pro-Arab leanings was finally healed. The Very Rev. Clarke MacDonald, Moderator a decade later, recalls that in the debate over whether Arabs or Israelis should hold Palestine, "Bruce fostered community with the Jewish people and also tried to maintain a human rights stance to the Arab people in Palestine."

What Bruce particularly recalls is meeting with Brazilian Archbishop Dom Helder Camara. Even though he had, by then, been in church delegations to the Middle East and Lebanon, it was Camara's blunt, simple talk which still stirs him. "You can go home," Camara told him. "We will solve these problems ourselves. If you'll just get off our back, it would help. If you would call on your business people to be as responsible when they operate in our part of the world as they are required by law to operate in your part of the world, if you would call on your governments to be as concerned for the welfare of the human family as they are for the welfare of their own constituents, that would be a big help."

For Bruce McLeod, that's one reason he has dedicated so much of his ministry to Canada. "I think I can do more here in this country, where I can speak the language. I go to those countries to remind myself of what I need to do here."

Bruce continues to hold Camara's words within himself. He brought them into the churches he held after being Moderator and he brings them into all his fields of interest.

Despite often being frustrated with the church, Bruce didn't follow others out of it in the 1960s. "One of the things that kept me in the church," he says, "was its continual lifting up of the whole world, the purpose of God's love. I knew that by being part of the church I could have my hands on bits of South Africa and South America and Asia in a way that I couldn't sitting alone in my kitchen, wringing my hands and responding to the spasmodic appeal of the radio."

He loved parts of the church, particularly the worship. What Camara called him to do fit perfectly with Bruce's idea of the purpose of worship's commissioning. "At the end of every service," he says, "you say, 'Go into the world' to the people who are the real ministers, the people who then go into the unions and the business meetings and the school rooms and the newspaper offices and fulfill their ministries. Those are the places where the decisions are made that will change our world. The minister, in a sense, is a step back from that. So, it's not surprising, then, for ministers to say, 'Hey, I'm going to come, too.' "

Camara's message fanned Bruce's own desire to be more a part of the world and he left Bloor Street United a year after he finished his term as Moderator. He spent a year working in Pueblito, Costa Rica as the first Canadian volunteer in a pilot project where private and public Canadian money was administered by a Costa Rican board to establish an agricultural cooperative and residential village for abandoned children. While there, Bruce says, "I learned so much, more than I could have learned here." With lifespans there so short, people freely embraced life's ups and downs and, he adds, there was a "simplicity, the ability to live now rather than planning for the weekend or next summer or when you retire."

He also delighted in living an entire year with no neckties and only two pairs of pants and three shirts. He missed his grand piano, on which he's noted for his singing and playing, but he valued the experiences. A decade later, though, he says, "I thought I'd learned that (lesson) forever, but I still value my grand piano and I have a drawer full of new shirts now. I've sort of fallen into this trap."

While in Costa Rica, Bruce was also a member of the Ontario Human Rights Commission — for which he returned to Canada for occasional meetings. After his Pueblito year, he worked full-time for the Commission for two years and chaired hearings across the province for revisions to the province's human rights code. The report, called "Life Together: A Report on Human Rights in Ontario", was presented to Ontario's government in 1977.

During that period, Bruce made more new discoveries. "I met people in human rights work who were knocking themselves out to make this place a province where people could live with each other in dignity and mutual respect," he says, "and who, almost without exception, had nothing to do with the church." Given that most of them were asking him why, as a minister, he was interested in justice and not just saving souls, he says, "I felt a mission to be there as a United Church minister, to embody the fact the church is interested in more than just building up its numbers and getting people into heaven. I also felt it was part of the work to build a society of people who are not discriminated against because of their membership in a minority group."

After serving on the Human Rights Commission, Bruce spent a year as the Liberal candidate for the east Toronto federal riding of the Beaches. He did that because someone asked him to and he believes everyone should be politically involved to encourage social and economic change. "Maybe you should miss a few church meetings and get involved with some candidate — that's mission," he says. But, he ran out of money before the election and went to work at Richmond Hill United. He ran again in 1980 as a Liberal candidate in the provincial election but lost to opponent Susan Fish, who put more time and money into the campaign.

"I grew up in Toronto, I'd been a minister in Toronto," he says, "but I learned more about this city in those five weeks than I ever had as a minister or a person growing up in Toronto. I was in rooms and places I never went to as a minister." One day he'd be in a very wealthy area where people had guard dogs and armed security guards would escort him into the houses. Next, he'd be in the basement room of a downtown hotel where he was greeted by a man in an undershirt surrounded by beer bottles. "As minister in Bloor Street or Metropolitan church, you don't normally go to these places," he says. "So, once again, I was meeting a world beyond the church."

After the election, Bruce worked at Richmond Hill United

until 1984 and Metropolitan United until mid-1987. He published a book of sermons, *City Sermons: Preaching from a Downtown Church*, and began writing regular columns for the Toronto *Star* on justice issues which range from Toronto's homeless to the strife in Haiti.

Through it all, he maintained and sharpened his feeling that the spirit of God is all about "trying to turn us into one family." Says Bruce, "The mission of the church is to become available to that purpose of God and that connection. The idea is not to turn everybody into Christians. That wouldn't please God particularly, to turn Hindus into Presbyterians. It's to listen to God's spirit as it has been moving in other religious communities, as it moves in people who aren't particularly religious at all, because God's spirit was here before any of us came." The challenge is to listen to others because every different view brings another thread of God to light. Then, the task is to help those who need it. "These are not ways of pleasing God," he says. "They're roads into the presence of God."

Bruce has tried to bring that message to his various parishioners. Reflecting on his most recent charge, he says, "The one little thing that I've done there is to try to open them up to God's work in the whole world, put them in touch with God's mission on the earth and not allow them to just look to their own growth. I really do try to make every part of the church (feel) part of that world-wide mission of God. (I) try and make that congregation intent not on its own survival or growth but on being available to that lively spirit that is still in the world. They shouldn't be so worried and busy all the time, they shouldn't be meeting in the church all the time, they should spend more time out in the community."

Bruce believes worship can show people "we're living in God's world and we're surrounded by that lively spirit that would blow through us and lift our hands up." Whether people decide to work in Brazil or right in their own community, that spirit lets them know they can help to heal the hurting condition of our world.

"You don't have to go far today," says Bruce. "There are lots of ways of tying into those conditions. Once you start to do it, of course, you're not going to rectify them immediately. But, there seems to be some sort of energy. It's as though you're in touch with some long movement in the world that is trying to make this a better place and that you, for a few years, are part of it. You won't achieve it, but your life energy will be aligned with that and you won't be wringing your hands anymore."

Bruce's message, and the way he delivers it, was appreciated by Toronto *Star* columnist Gary Lautens. Lautens attended Metropolitan and subsequently introduced Bruce to the *Star's* publisher, who hired him to write a regular column. "He's the best preacher I've ever heard in this country," says Lautens, noting that his message is passionate but intelligent. "Bruce is absolutely one of the best for his combination of humility, intellect, passion and technical skills — all the things you look for in the church. He has a crusade in life, but he doesn't just stand up and harangue you. He also doesn't just sit back and look. He gets very involved, goes out on the street and knows what is happening there. I don't find any hypocrisy in him."

Bruce's message is also heard, and needed, in the wider United Church, says former Moderator MacDonald. "I see Bruce as a person who is highly motivated by a sense of justice which comes from his faith base. The indignation about oppression which he communicates in his columns in the *Star* or wherever he writes or speaks derives from his sense of God as justice." MacDonald credits Bruce for realizing that "if you hold strong views about something and if you're going to impact society, you cannot avoid the political arena."

Beyond that, MacDonald notes, "Bruce doesn't mind using the needle when it needs to be used to prick people to attention about things. We need people who'll raise our consciousness about all things we may be unconscious of or apathetic about."

Bruce feels his sense of mission fits with The United Church of Canada. He cites a 1966 stand where the church "finally came to the position officially that God is redemptively at work in all religious life." He applauds the recognition by his church that it isn't the only instrument of God's mission and that it must be "ready to co-operate with other instruments of God's mission, whether they be other religions or other people." As for the church, he says it's important as a vehicle for "really telling the story of the faith. We remember this is God's world and we remind ourselves to break the bread, take the wine and go out and join those good people who don't apparently need this reminder."

As to how successful the United Church is at living out what Bruce sees to be its mission, he says, "We have our moments... We all work at making it as good as it can be." While the church's form of doing mission may have changed, he believes it has always struggled to be available to God's spirit. It's a history he's proud of and in which he feels comfortable. He's particularly pleased with the church's lobbying of the federal government against a refugee bill which would bar refugees from Canada and it's calling for human rights legislation which demands people of all colours, sexual orientations and ages be treated equally as God's children. "The United Church's involvement in those sorts of social and political issues is very much the mission of the church," he says.

As for those who criticize such stands, Bruce says, "I rejoice in the variety (of opinions). I think that, at most, any of us only have a glimpse of God's reality." But, even while he lauds varying opinions because they challenge him to better explore and explain his own beliefs, he adds, "it's not that everybody has to agree with a stand on a given political issue, but you have to agree with the need for justice. From basic issues of justice, there can be no compromise. There could be, in my view, no United Church person who says a homosexual person has no right to be in the United Church."

It's a powerful message and one many may find hard to digest. But, then Bruce has given his life to a very non-traditional ministry, weaving in and out of churches and the world. He acknowledges, "I've had more opportunities than anybody deserves and I haven't always made the best of them. But, I look forward to more chances. I've always tried to go through as many doors as I could because I think none of us are here for very long. Other people are different, but I would be so frustrated if I spent all my life in one place, just having tasted one kind of experience. The whole world is God's world and I'm restless because I haven't been to India or South Africa and I want to go."

Bruce tries to follow his Costa Rican lessons by enjoying what life offers now rather than planning too far ahead. Still, he has plans for a trip to a Pueblito project in Brazil with his new wife, Rev. Joyce Kelly, and he thrills to all sorts of future possibilities. "I just think the world is a wonderful place and it keeps beckoning me," he says. "So I'm just looking forward to whatever surprises there are down the road and hoping I have the energy and health to be available."

PEGGY MONAGUE:
LEADER AND BRIDGE BUILDER

by Mike Milne

From the end of the street where Peggy Monague lives with her husband, Neil, and her four children, you can see a small patch of Penetang Harbour, which wends its circuitous way out to Georgian Bay. To the east and south, unseen, lies Midland Bay. These waters, in the 17th century, carried the first European settlers into this part of what's now Ontario. It was on the shores of these protected bays that French fur traders and Jesuit missionaries set about the economic exploitation and "Christianization" of the Huron Indians.

Today, there are no Huron Indians in these parts. Their contact with the Jesuit missionaries brought European-style Christianity to some of them and European diseases to all of them. Within a little more than a decade, smallpox, diphtheria and wars with the Iroquois (fuelled by conflict between the British and French empires) had decimated the Huron nation.

All that remains of the Hurons today in the Midland-Penetanguishene area of Ontario is a small reconstruction of one of their villages, a considerably larger reconstruction of the Jesuits' village — Ste.-Marie Among the Hurons— and a huge Roman Catholic shrine to the eight martyrs who died bringing Christianity to the Hurons.

The native people who live in the area today are primarily Ojibways. Among them, Peggy Monague is searching, amid the cultural wreckage of well-meaning Christian mission, for a distinctly native approach to Christianity.

The Monague house is much like its modern, suburban neighbors— brick and aluminum, with patches of lawn front and back. There are two late-model cars in the driveway and inside there's a warm and welcome kitchen, redolent of fresh-brewed coffee. One end of the kitchen table is laden with several files, the telephone is ready at hand and there's a well-thumbed, modern translation of the Bible nearby. Peggy Monague, a young native woman, is well into the morning's work.

There's a more formal office downstairs, complete with filing cabinets, a desk and typewriters   but, with her two youngest children at day care and her two teenage daughters at school, she finds the bright kitchen more inviting. Peggy works as a regional coordinator for the Ontario-Quebec Native Council of The United Church of Canada. She came on staff in 1987, but has worked as a volunteer for several years.

Like any active church body, the Council has its seemingly endless meetings, its mounds of paperwork, its bookkeeping and administration, its disputes and diplomacy. It also has a mandate to look at what it means to move toward the creation of a presbytery encompassing the 22 native United churches of Ontario and Quebec.

Looking back at all its years of heavy-handed "evangelism" and blatant paternalism towards native people, the United Church made a formal apology during the Sudbury General Council meeting in 1986. There's now an opening, a point of light, in the bleak history of relations between the largely white, culturally European church and Canada's original people. In that point of light stands Peggy Monague, along with the other native people who are willing to give the United Church a second chance.

Peggy was born and grew up on the Rama Reserve, on the shores of long, narrow Lake Couchiching, just north of Orillia, Ontario. She was "about in the middle" of a family of nine children. Her mother, Dora Benson, a devout and respected elder of the Rama United Church, saw to it that her family went to church. "At that time, we had to go to church and be quiet to sing in the choir," says Peggy with a smile. Later on, after piano lessons, she switched to organ and played in the church.

There was public school in Orillia, then high school (including a year in Kitchener, funded as part of an obscure "experiment" by the Department of Indian Affairs), then community college (two years of medical secretary training). There was a first marriage to a Metis and the birth of two daughters, Laura and Tina, now teenagers. There was an accounting job in Orillia, government work and a university course in native economic development and small business management.

Peggy met Neil Monague, an Ojibway from Christian Island, near Penetanguishene, Ontario, five years ago at the funeral of a mutual friend from Rama and they were married a year later. Peggy and Neil have since added two new members to the family: two-year-old Kathleen and one-year-old Whitney.

After finishing school, Peggy worked and raised her children, but she left behind the baggage of her United Church upbringing. Or at least she thought she had.

"I didn't bother with the church when I was in my 20s," she says. (She's now in her 30s.) "I didn't bother. I had left the reserve and went out and did my own thing—just to find out what I wanted to do."

She lost her Ojibway language, too, at an early age— about the time she and the other children from Rama began to ride the bus to school in Orillia. She wasn't brought up with native culture or native spirituality but, rather, with the culture of the "conqueror" and the religion of the missionaries. Still, she never lost the notion that she mattered as a person and, at a certain point, she began to feel that she may have been missing something, some part of herself.

"We were brought up in white society, so the way you're brought up is the way you believe.... But, about five years ago, I started to learn about native culture."

This new aspect of Peggy's education began at Trent University in Peterborough, Ontario, where she was taking a course with other native people. One day, two traditional native elders came into the class to perform a sweetgrass ceremony. It was one of those rituals, part of the traditional native system of beliefs, which missionaries had worked long and hard to suppress. Peggy, herself, had been warned about these rituals and told to steer clear.

"I knew from my upbringing that I wasn't supposed to become involved," she says. "And I was really leery. I didn't know what to do. Should I stay or should I go out? If I left I would offend the traditional leaders who were doing the ceremony. So I asked the girl next to me what I should do— should I stay or should I go? She said, 'Do whatever you feel you should do.' So I stayed and it was from that time on that I had a lot of struggling."

It was a critical struggle for Peggy to find a spiritual path she could follow. It had to be a path which would honor the feelings that led her to take part in the sweetgrass ceremony. But, it also had to honour her Christian upbringing and her strong faith in God. Peggy's brush with   native spirituality had raised a beacon of promise, a desire for a fuller spiritual life, but she found that her personal path led back to the Christian church.

Back at Rama, in the late 1970s, she began to attend church again. But, at the same time, she began to look critically at the way "the system" works against the right of native people to take charge of their own lives.

"I had come back to the church," says Peggy. "This was what I wanted. But, I couldn't accept what was."

"What was" at Rama, as at most other native churches, was a continuing kind of missionary-style paternalism, which the United Church had supposedly tried to shed in the mid-1960s when it dismantled the old Home Missions Board. (The Board used to both own and, effectively, operate "mission" churches, such as native and ethnic congregations.) Rama was part of a three-point pastoral charge, along with two non-native churches. Although Rama was represented on the Official Board of the charge, native people tended to stand back and let non-natives run things.

"The native people really didn't have a say, or they didn't push for it," says Peggy. "I couldn't understand how they could just sit back."

Peggy has always been one to stand up for herself, to assert her right to respect and her right to live and express herself as a native Canadian. She says she was raised to believe that she was just as good and just the same as other people. While, early on, that may have limited her expression as a native (for a long time she didn't see that she was any different from non-native people), it always gave her the strength to stand up for herself.

Peggy first encountered open prejudice against natives in Kitchener, where she boarded with a minister's family while taking Grade 12. A boy called her a "squaw" and she wouldn't let him go until he showed some repentence. They both got into trouble for being late for class, but Peggy had made her point. There have been other incidences of racism, she says, and they've hurt deeply.

But, the institutional racism of the United Church,

hidden under a veneer of benevolence, was something the young woman could do something about, something she could work on personally. At Rama, she joined the church's Official Board and got involved with other natives who were working nationally through the Native Ministries Council. Her experience with that group, with people already part of native presbyteries, helped give her more confidence and more knowledge of how the United Church works. This is knowledge from which natives have traditionally been shielded, first by the Home Missions Board and later by a more low-key paternalism.

Soon after Peggy got back into the thick of things at Rama, the church decided to go on its own as a single-point charge. The result was that Rama became a much more active church.

"That's why I always speak of Rama, because they've gone ahead and done things," says Peggy. "The community became involved then, whereas before the community wasn't involved with the church. Everything was done for the native people, you know. The ministers were sent there, the money was looked after and the people thought, well, they're all right, they're looked after anyway." Still officially a member at Rama, Peggy also attends the Christian Island church whenever she can, sometimes playing the organ at weddings, funerals or other occasions.

The changes at Rama have been part and parcel of a dramatic shift across the United Church during the past decade. Native churches have faced and dealt with their need for native ministry and personnel, their desire for autonomy and the need to address and deal with past injustices.

With the development of unique native ministry training programs, the churches are now well on the way toward developing a pool of native ministers. With the creation of two native presbyteries (so far) and a native Conference, the churches have been able to realize their need for structural autonomy. And, with the United Church's formal apology to native people at the Sudbury General Council, today's native church has been able both to see the church's recognition of past faults and hear its promise of a liberated future.

It looks good at a glance and, certainly, the church liberals should be happy. But, beyond the sincere platitudes, there's still lots of bridge-building work to be done.

"It's going to take a long time," says Peggy, wrapping her

hands around another warm cup of coffee. "The United Church may have apologized. But, General Council apologized, it's not the people. It didn't come from the congregations, from the people themselves. They still have a long way to go."

Many native people and communities have a long way to go, too, before they'll be free of the dependence into which the old paternalism has lulled them. Dependence is like addiction. As long as you're getting what you need, complacency reigns. But, when needs aren't met and conditions change, there's a difficult period of withdrawal.

The addiction comparison is easy for Peggy and Neil Monague to appreciate. Peggy says she grew up in an alcoholic family and Neil, an alcoholic, stopped drinking only four years ago, shortly after meeting Peggy.

Neil talks freely about "the man I put on the shelf four years ago." It's a man, says Neil, who could come down again if not watched carefully. He quit drinking, cold turkey, one New Year's Eve. "I put down the bottle and that was it." But, afterwards, it got rough. "It's like riding a boat. There's a lot of waves but the boat doesn't tip. It was a rocky situation for the first six months. Every time we'd pass a tavern, I'd look at it and say, 'I should be in there.' But, she (Peggy) really helped me."

Another thing that helps Neil, as well as his wry sense of humour, is his recent exploration and discovery of native culture, his Ojibway heritage. Through a job as a native "interpreter" at Ste.-Marie Among the Hurons for the past two years, Neil has met some natives who are following the traditional spiritual path. Part of his cultural rediscovery has involved craft work. Neil makes beautiful, fire-blackened clay pipes and hand-carved stone pipes.

While Peggy is working, slowly and carefully, at incorporating her native traditions into Christianity, Neil tends to look more towards the traditional native ways. "I can't say I'm traditional yet. I've just got my foot in the door of the culture because it's not something I grew up on," he says. "I'm just wanting to learn something about who my people are, what they were and what I want to be."

So far, the couple has managed to compromise well. There are signs of that around the house: braided sweetgrass hangs in the living room and there's an eagle's feather as protection for the house. The parallel paths they've taken have collided a few times. But, says Neil, "I think we've gone through the stormy part of it now."

The word "mission" doesn't stir warm feelings for many native people. They've felt patronized, pigeon-holed and put down by the "mission churches" created, for the most part, by "well-meaning" whites. It makes it hard for native people to talk about how they see *their* mission within the church. Often, they prefer to substitute words like "Christian development" for "mission".

"When I think of mission, I think of submission," says Neil Monague forcefully. "The people submitted to the church... That's how I feel."

In moving from submission to true Christian mission, in seeing God working through them, instead of over them or at them, native people are now taking cues from their own traditional ways. Instead of Robert's Rules of Order, they use consensus-building, instead of the hierarchy, there is the circle.

For Peggy, that means accepting leadership within the church, but leading by example: showing, not telling. It means a willingness to take chances. It means an unwillingness to accept things the way they are and a challenge to make the journeys and have the adventures that will bring about growth and change.

It's like the time she spent a year in Kitchener as a teenager, part of that long-forgotten government experiment. "I always see things as an adventure," says Peggy. "And it was, too."

So, too, is the work of the United Church in the area of native ministries. Without question, Peggy Monague has the self-confidence and self-assurance to both carry on her role as co-ordinator and work out a spiritual place for herself in the United Church. However, as with the rest of us, acceptance and assurance by other church people also means a great deal to her.

"When I hear the drums, I can just feel it within myself— the nativeness— something really special and deep. If I can't feel that and if I can't believe in that in Christianity— how can you stop the native person from feeling the spirituality, from letting that come out?

"I have a lot of respect, I have a deep sense of serenity and peace of mind, knowing our culture is very sacred and very special."

The Christian church has come a long way since 1639 when the Jesuits set up their village at Ste. Marie. But, it also has a long way to go to ensure that the mistakes of the past don't poison the future.

Says Peggy, "I really enjoy this work, because it goes a long way back."

BOB HAVERLUCK:
PRAIRIE COMIC,
PRAIRIE PROPHET

by Jo-Ann Roberts Kelly

Bob Haverluck is described by one of his friends as a "reluctant prophet". He's also described as "outrageous". In keeping with the great biblical tradition of the prophets, both descriptions fit.

Bob responds to God's call through the medium of comic art. There's something about a Haverluck cartoon that makes it instantly recognizable, whether it's in *Harper's*, the United Church *Observer* or on an art gallery wall. Like *Peanuts* by Schultz or *Herman* by Unger, it has a style all its own. Of course, not everyone likes the Haverluck style. What they particularly don't like is that a Haverluck cartoon can leave you feeling a bit uncomfortable.

That doesn't bother Bob Haverluck, an ordained United Church minister who has chosen to devote his time to cartooning. His "playfully grotesque" figures serve many purposes for Bob. He says his characters reflect "the holy earthiness of creation. I purposefully inflate their bodies so there is no escaping the earthly quality of them. It allows me to take my message and my ministry to the reality of where people are."

Bob compares his cartoon ministry to his other favourite form of ministry — visiting. "It takes me to people's kitchen tables where life is most real. My ministry is to try and draw out the comedy and earthiness of our life together."

In a series of cartoons for Advent and Christmas, drawn for the *Observer*, critics were upset because Mary looked "like a child with Down's Syndrome." But, Bob says there is intentionally a shock value in what he draws. "If my Mary causes someone to realize that Mary doesn't have to have a white gown, a blue shawl and a model's figure, then maybe they will realize that Mary was a woman just like them. She is someone they can identify with. For some people, there is no way they can relate to Mary as a goddess."

Bob Haverluck, born in 1945, has been a bit of a rebel for most of his life. He, himself, admits he has a "disruptive nature" but he also points out that he tries to "disrupt the right things."

He grew up in Dauphin, Manitoba and became a candidate for the United Church ministry in grade eleven. That was also the year he and his best friend were asked to leave high school."We were told if we didn't leave that we would be kicked out." Bob says the request came about because of "youthful exuberance" and his rebellion against the "authoritarianism of some teachers." He and his friend left that school and Dauphin, Manitoba behind. Bob was 16 years old.

His very close friend and colleague, Rev. Paul Campbell, says he thinks what really happened was that Bob "kind of outgrew the place and needed more reality to push against."

Another person who remembers Bob from his early high school days is Dr. Tom Axworthy, a former political advisor to Prime Minister Pierre Trudeau. Axworthy says he can remember being at a Boys Parliament in Winnipeg when he was in grade nine or ten. "There was this bright kid from Dauphin, wearing a great, blue sports coat. He gave a very solicitous and very funny speech. With my Winnipeg arrogance, I thought isn't this something that someone from Dauphin is the best-dressed and most entertaining speaker here." Their paths were to cross again.

Why would such a young rebel, albeit one with eloquent speech and quick wit, feel called to ordained ministry? Bob says he wasn't "a church rat." He came from a "nominal United Church family" that went to church most Sundays. "I went to Sunday School and some youth groups but I didn't hang around the church. In fact, I hung out in Dauphin at places where I would meet the characters— the pool halls and restaurants of the town. However, some of the most real and unreal people I knew were in the church."

Campbell remembers that during one of his visits to the Haverluck home he saw a picture of five-year-old Bob and his brother. He says, "What was amazing was the look in Bob's eye. He looked unbelievably wise and precocious for his age. It was as if you could see his soul." Campbell adds that the look is still in Bob's eyes. Even as a youngster, he says, Bob had a reputation for being an inquisitive little boy who would talk to anyone, was interested in everything and asked lots of questions.

Bob Haverluck, in his intellectual and spiritual journey, came to see that exposing false authority is a prophetic task. While he doesn't put himself in the same league as Jonah and Jeremiah, he uses them as early examples of this role. He also points out that it's not a task most people would want, including himself. In fact, he says being called to this task, as he feels he is, often seems like a curse.

"The task is troubling. Everyone sees a place for it but no one wants to be responsible for it— sort of like being a garbage man. It's definitely not everyone's vocation. Seeing the wrong and feeling compelled to show it to others does not feel like a virtue. I wish I didn't have an eye for those things. But, then, there's a part of me that is sheer play and wants to sing and dance."

Bob's friends have no trouble seeing him as a modern-day prophet— if at times a misunderstood one. In fact, at a farewell party organized when he was stepping down as co-director of the Prairie Christian Training Centre (PCTC), his friends did a skit that had Bob as Jonah in the belly of the whale.

Like the prophets he identifies with, Bob admits that he's a vessel, a vehicle for God. He says he doesn't have much of a sense that what he's doing is coming from himself. He also stresses that he's in no way above the vices he portrays in his art. "I am able to portray them because I recognize them and can identify them as part of myself."

Says Campbell, "Bob is driven by a biblical vision that life ought to be better. There must be more justice and hope." He describes Bob as a very funny person who could be very popular because of his humour. However, "Bob never plays to the crowd. It seems there's always a point where there's a parting of the ways. He ends up delighting some people, who think he's brilliant, and disgusting others."

As an example of this, he tells the story of a roast that was organized when the Executive Secretary of (then) Manitoba Conference, Ernie Johnston, retired in 1975. "Bob knew and liked Ernie and was giving an absolutely hilarious depiction of Ernie's career, parodying all he had done. The audience was eating out of his hand and, then, out of the blue, Bob says, 'Shortly after that, Ernie started his ministry to hemorrhoid sufferers.' You could see that only a few people were enjoying the joke— the rest were sorry they could still hear him."

His critics dismiss Bob with the remark that he's just a guy who never grew up. When you first meet him, you might think there's some truth to that statement. With his wire- rim "granny glasses", soft flannel shirts, casual cords, big wool socks and sandal-style slippers, there's a temptation to peg him as a '60s hippy who hasn't joined the yuppy generation of the '80s. But, that conclusion would be wrong.

Bob, because of his calling, isn't likely to be totally in step with any generational trend. He responds to different influences. Even though he lives in Winnipeg, there's a strong sense of rural values and presence. That's not accidental. Bob says he chooses to live in the north end of Winnipeg because it's most like living in the country.

He's not a serene person. You can sense his anger and frustration with a world that seems intent on refusing the good things God has created for it. And yet, he's not an overgrown adolescent lashing out at the world, either. There's a tremendous depth to Bob Haverluck in the way he thinks and works in the context of a broken and suffering world. He has travelled a long way since the days when he was "encouraged" to find another high school.

Paul Campbell notes that a lot of people simply don't understand Bob. They don't realize he has this deep-rooted faith which is the base of everything he says and does. "He has an unusual mind and is really gifted with his ability to see things differently than others. He is also a very thoughtful person. I can't imagine not having him for a friend."

Bob admits that, for such a serious thinker, his saving grace is having a sense of play. He credits his mother for giving him an appreciation of the comic. His father, a small town businessman, was a "verbal cartoonist who had a wonderful memory for stories." In addition, his parents were very honest, down-to-earth people who taught Bob to see the value in everybody.

His godmother was a Roman Catholic, which Bob feels gave him an early introduction to ecumenism. He says the theology he learned at home was a spoken theology. It may not have been doctrinal or religious training at its best, but it did give him a sense of how important it was to care about God's world. The form was there, if not all the content.

The content would come after he left Dauphin for Winnipeg in 1960. He finished his secondary education there and went on to the University of Winnipeg where he earned a bachelor of arts. This led to a brief career as a high school teacher in Cranberry Portage, Manitoba. He then did a year of study in philosophy at the University of Toronto and three years of theology at the University of Winnipeg after which he was ordained by the Manitoba Conference of the United Church in 1971.

Following his ordination, Bob and his wife, Gerry, went to England for two years so he could do a doctoral program in theology and culture at the University of Lancaster. While in England, he and Gerry lived in a Quaker community near the university. It was there that Bob worked at further defining his idea of mission and exploring the role of the comic.

In the Quaker community, he says, mission was something that happened between people. It wasn't what someone did for someone else. "Mission is not a question of someone possessing something and handing it out. It's what happens when people come together with an openness about giving away what they have— not selling it or exchanging it— but letting give and take happen. The truth kind of emerges in that process and God's face is shown. The mission comes through the meeting and, if there is no meeting, there is no mission."

He adds that mission is also receiving. He uses his own example to prove the point. "There is no drawing, no comedy that doesn't begin from somewhere else. It may bubble up from inside me in one sense, but it's only because I've received it in another sense from meeting people, from being part of different communities. It's one of the ways that God and the Holy Spirit show forth through the daily encounters. These meetings are not necessarily pleasant. Grace can emerge from horrible realities."

Bob tells the story of how one drawing of Jesus kissing a pig came to be. He was looking after a two-year-old boy, Andrew, as a favour for a friend. He and Andrew were out playing when the little boy pointed to a tree and asked, "What's that?" Bob said, "A tree," and Andrew ran to it and hugged it and kissed it. He repeated this with a rock and again the child ran and kissed it.

Suddenly, Bob had an image of Jesus embracing things indiscriminately as Andrew was doing and, by so doing, sanctifying and purifying them. When he returned to his drafting table, that image became the drawing of Jesus kissing a pig.

The cartoons and whimsical drawings started seriously in 1983. Bob had just completed six years as co-director of the Prairie Christian Training Centre. He was at Shoal Lake Pastoral Charge and was "tired of hearing my own voice." He'd taught clowning for a while but felt it wasn't as easily used as a teaching tool. So, he was looking for another means of expression.

Bob never really considered himself an artist. Up until that point, his art was limited to doodling at meetings, illustrating children's stories on Sundays or making little sketches to facilitate prayer. One day, the doodlings from a meeting reminded him of cartoons he enjoyed and he started to go to some of his favourites in search of a style. He always liked the *New Yorker* magazine's cartoons. They had figures with bones but no flesh. As it turned out, the Haverluck style would be just the opposite.

Another long-time friend, Rev. Ian MacDonald, notes that Bob has always succeeded at whatever he's done, whether it be rural ministry, PCTC, writing, teaching or cartooning. He says Bob has a "creativity, an edge, an insight. He is also very life-giving to those he meets." However, MacDonald admits that Bob has always chosen a different path for himself.

Unfortunately, says MacDonald, "we (in the church) don't know how to use him... If the church or the universities were more creative in finding a way to use Bob's talents, his life would have been a lot easier these past few years. No one seems to have a role for a prophet, an artist and clown."

From the very beginning of his ministry, Bob has been sensitive to and involved with peace and justice groups. However, he felt that people in these movements tended to work very hard with very little laughter. He wanted to help them discover play, so Bob decided to become their "jester".

MacDonald says Bob knew how common and damaging burn-out could be to those working for peace, social justice and other faith issues. "He'd seen burn-out in himself and he wanted to find a way to keep the weary radicals alive."

Bob's first drawings were used as illustrations for a slide

show on nuclear issues. From that experience, the work has grown. His cartoons have appeared in *Harper's Magazine,* the *New Statesman, Christian Century* , the *National Catholic Reporter* and the United Church *Observer* . He has held art gallery shows and has illustrated a book on the *ABC's of Peace.* Haverluck drawings can also show up where you least expect them: in offices, behind the counter at stores or tacked to a bulletin board in a peace group's office.

The last location is probably the one which would please Bob the most. He wants his artistic message to get around. "One thing about my art is that it's a popular art form that's easily xeroxed," he says. "I very seldom work in colors for that very reason. I want people to be able to use my work and share it with others cheaply."

The United Church *Observer* is one of the primary users of Bob's art in Canada. Says managing editor Muriel Duncan, "Bob sends us a lot more work than we can print, but we really enjoy getting his packages. We often pass them around the office. He always has something important to say. His particular approach strips away all pretense. He does this so effectively that he offends some people. But, he does help us see ourselves."

Duncan points out that the *Observer* always gets a reaction to Bob's work. The greatest response, both for and against, is when they run his depictions of well known biblical figures, where there's already an artistic image in people's minds.

His Christmas series with Mary and the naked shepherds was a case in point. The negative response was swift. "I have never seen a more grotesque attempt at depicting any part of the Christmas story.....I find them neither funny nor art...a sacrilege of the most disgusting form...hideous...disgusting," the letters said.

According to Duncan, the positive response is usually a bit slower in coming and it tends to react to the negative letters. Those who liked the Haverluck article and accompanying illustrations said, "Don't these people read the text?....thank-you, thank-you for that liberating article...as a new mother I can identify with the image of a pregnant Mary....it allows us to realize that God makes beautiful the seemingly imperfect even at the risk of challenging impropriety and conventionality." In the text accompanying his Christmas drawings, Bob cut to the heart of the matter: "What if God becomes human in ways that we find unattractive, unlike us or even ugly?"

Bob Haverluck knows very well that some people will be upset by his art, but he feels his work should be a tool for popular education on values and issues. He's particularly focussed on peace and justice concerns. One drawing, entitled "The Stars and Stripes in Central America", shows a weary and battered person bound by stripes of wire with star-shaped barbs. It's a powerful statement about American involvement in Central America.

A sensitive, almost poetic, use of words is very much a part of Bob's art and ministry. In an article on angels which appeared in the *Observer* in September, 1986, he depicts angels as having feet bigger than their wings. The drawings are playful, but certainly unlike any traditional angelic image. And, that's exactly the point. In the text he says, "What is most amusing is our looking to sunlit clouds for messengers of the Holy, while often they are working near us in the everyday or entering our lives as dusky strangers. Because their feet are often bigger than their wings and they have more faults than feathers, we are tempted to think 'no Holy word could come from here.' "

Together with Anne Szumigalski, Bob has written a liturgy entitled *Prairie Mass* which responds to the natural elements of the prairie: wheat and weather, crocus and lily. In it, the story of Jesus and his disciples arguing over who will be the first in heaven is re-done as a Braggart's Play about the opening of the west. By combining scripture and poetry, hymns and original music, it makes liturgy a popular art form.

But, where in the organized church does a person find a place when his or her sense of mission and service has led to drawing pictures and writing words that aren't always under- stood or appreciated?

Bob says it's hard not to have an official place in the church structure. There's no job description for what he does. But, he feels God calls people out of one community and into other communities. It's for this sense of place and belonging that Bob values the informal communities in which he's involved. During the past eight years he has been part of a "house church", a group of 16 people from the United and Roman Catholic churches who gather one evening a month in small groups for worship and Bible study.

Bob and Gerry were married in 1968. They have no children of their own but they have an extended family of friends with small children. Gerry is described by her friends as a woman with a very fine mind and a quick wit — which serves to make the Haverlucks a well-matched couple. Gerry devotes a lot of her energy to her work with the North End Community Ministry in Winnipeg. She's also a big supporter of Bob's efforts to express his faith and mission through art.

The Haverlucks live in a heritage home on the Red River. Bob sits in the bay window of their front room, perched on a stool facing a blank sheet of paper on his drafting table. As he looks out at the river beyond the trees, he reflects on his art.

"In the art community, comic art is seen as a marginal art form. There aren't many grants. It's seen as 'just cartoons'," he says. "Our understanding of this art is not as rich as it is of other areas. Comedy is a rich medium but, in our culture, comedy is the sit-com."

"Biblical comedy is meant for meditation," he adds. "Within the church there's a need for a greater understanding of the complexity of human nature. Liturgy and the arts must be supported to a greater degree."

Bob points out that the United Church isn't the main user of his work overall. His cartoons frequently appear in Catholic publications, both in Canada and the United States, as well as church and political magazines in England, Scotland and Sweden. He also sells some of his work to the public, but he won't sell a piece unless it's been copied.

Ian MacDonald tells a story about an art exhibition Bob had in his home town of Dauphin. When he was pricing his work for sale, Bob put high prices (or what he considered high) on the drawings he really didn't want to sell. To his amazement, they were the first to go.

Will Bob Haverluck still be drawing in five years? "I hope so," he says. "But, if there's no place for me and my art, then I'll do something else." He doesn't want to completely cut his links with pastoral ministry because he doesn't want to lose touch with the grassroots community which has fed his spirit for so long.

Ian MacDonald predicts that in 15 years Bob's material will be widely used and published and everybody who ever knew him will be telling everybody else how they loved his work long before he became famous.

Bob and his circle of friends are, clearly, very important to one another. Tom Axworthy has been a friend since their early days in Boys Parliament. They met again at United College (now the University of Winnipeg). Bob's first official ministerial act after he was ordained was to marry Tom and his wife, Roberta. Later, the two couples found themselves in England doing post-graduate studies at the same time. Says Axworthy, "I know Haverluck is not everybody's cup of tea, but he certainly is mine."

Axworthy says he has always admired Bob's intelligence, social commitment and idealism. When he was serving as a policy advisor to the prime minister, he says he'd often call Bob to discuss issues with him. "We didn't always agree, but I always valued what he had to say."

MacDonald says, "It's true what someone once said about Bob. He has no initial charisma, but of all the people I know in the church no one has a way of coming through in the long-run like Bob." There are times, he adds, when he would "cheerfully throttle him for always having to be so honest." But, the positive side is that Bob is very much a teacher who is always willing to share his knowledge and insights with his friends.

"You can be working on a sermon and Bob will drop by for coffee," says MacDonald. "He'll casually point out that your approach is the standard interpretation but, then, he'll show you a different approach. It's always biblically sound and usually better than what you started with."

Campbell says Bob's willingness to share himself with others isn't limited to a small group. "He's a very thoughtful pastor and friend," he says. "Often, after a visit, Bob will drop in again with a copy of an article or a book that relates to something you mentioned in your earlier meeting. He's always feeding people."

In keeping with his understanding of mission, Bob feels just as strongly that his friends and the people he meets also feed him. The real people in the church, he says, are the small clusters who work on the mission of the church. He has always worked closely with these people on his pastoral charges at Shoal Lake, Morden, Darlingford, Pearce, Thornhill and at the Prairie Christian Training Centre. "I want to write about them and support them," he says, "because they are the ones who have kept me in the church, tied to them and their wit, their long-suffering patience and their passion for spiritual well-being."

Bob admits his skills aren't best-used doing administrative work. He feels he can contribute by offering comic relief to those who are often swamped by administrative detail. "I want them to laugh. I want to amuse them."

He does amuse them and lots of other people as well, but not all the time. Like the prophets of old, he must face scorn and ridicule in his attempt to preach the truth. But, it's his sense of play which makes him special. Tom Axworthy says it this way: "I've known lots of philosophers and lots of social activists. None of them make me laugh...but Bob does." You get the impression that God enjoys a joke once in a while, too.

MARY HAGGART: GRASSROOTS PASTOR WITH A GLOBAL SPIRIT

by Deana Driver

She grew up through a depression and a war and she spent seven years of young adulthood working as a domestic servant for little pay and even less recognition. But, during the hard times, she always had a sense that God was present to offer help and strength.

From these beginnings — because of these beginnings — Mary Haggart, born in Ottawa in 1920 of a labourer father and housewife mother, has dedicated the last 40 years to helping others achieve their own potential both here and abroad.

As a United Church minister, she has worked at all levels of the church, in everything from Christian education to outreach and mission. She was co-founder of a dynamic Ten Days For World Development group in Saskatchewan and has served on the Conference and national divisions of World Outreach. She has had an important impact on her church and community.

Mary Haggart was raised in Brockville, Ontario through the 1920s and '30s. She recalls that her family was like most other families of the period — dirt poor. She loved the outdoors, with all its beauty and freedom, and came to be known as a tomboy.

When she was in Grade 4, one of her teachers told her she had the capabilities to go on to university. It was a sentiment that would be repeated by another instructor in Grade 8. For Mary, it became a dream that wouldn't die.

"It was my father's dream for himself," she says. "I guess I sort of inherited it. He wasn't educated. He wanted to write." Mary was the oldest of seven children and one of her daily duties was to teach her father what she'd learned at school that day.

At age 15, Mary left home to take work as a domestic

servant. "When you're in domestic service, you work for everybody, but you never have any say," she says. "You become a shy little person. You're a nobody."

By age 21, she had made up her mind to get some further training, so she went to night school and enlisted in the Canadian Women's Army Corps the following year. It was an exhilarating feeling to discover her own abilities through the army, says Mary. "I could lead. I could do things. I was somebody."

She served in the army until 1946, when she took advantage of the opportunity for educational upgrading. She entered the University of Western Ontario and received her bachelor's degree in general arts in 1950.

It was a difficult time for Mary and she called on her family for support. She recalls one particular occasion when her father's words were an inspiration to her. She was worried about school and told him she didn't think she'd ever make it out of Western.

"He said, 'You'll make it and you'll do whatever you want to do,'" recalls Mary with a smile. "They didn't always understand me, but they were there," she says of her parents. Her father died while she was at Western and her mother died in 1986.

About the time she received her degree, Mary joined The United Church of Canada. "I wanted to have my life count for something and I wanted to write," she says. "So I tried to put those two things together and found myself in the United Church Training School in Toronto (now the Centre for Christian Studies).

However, there was no space for full-time writers within the church and Mary didn't want to be a deaconess or a missionary, the positions for which she was being trained. "I just felt that wasn't where I was at, what I was supposed to be." She spent hours in prayer and thought, considering her future. Eventually, she went to the session at Empress Church in London, Ontario to seek approval to become a candidate for ordained ministry. It was a step she took reluctantly.

"I didn't want to do it," says Mary matter-of-factly. "I didn't want to be a minister, but this was where I was being pulled to. I would have been happy with my typewriter in a small room."

She "hoped to heaven" the church would tell her to forget it. But, they didn't. "When I did go to the session and I was accepted as a candidate, I knew a great deal of joy. So I knew I was on the right track," Mary says now.

She graduated from training school in 1952 and from Toronto's Emmanuel College in 1954.

Right from the beginning, Mary had to defend her choice of profession. "The night I was being ordained, my mother said, 'You've always been a tomboy, Mary, and now you're going into a man's profession,'" she recalls. "I argued it wasn't a man's profession. It was for both men and women. Then she asked me, 'Will you ever be able to wear jeans again?' and I said, 'I don't see why not.' She was happy."

Mary wanted her first pastorate to be in Alberta. Instead, she was settled at Cabri, Saskatchewan, a town of 700 people about 65 kilometres north of Swift Current. Her first experience of life in a rural charge was arriving at Cabri and not being able to make it to the manse because her car was stuck in the gumbo. "One of the first things I was taught was how to drive in that stuff," she says with a laugh.

There had been about 10 female ministers in Saskatchewan before Mary, but she still had to learn how to do ministry as a woman and convince others of her capabilities.

"There was always the struggle of the balance between being aggressive and being warm and friendly," she says. "For a long time, Lydia Gruchy and I were the only ones (female ministers in the province)."

"For about the first 10 years of my ministry, I was sick every Sunday morning," she says. "Breakfast made a two-way trip. Talk about being nervous." However, she knows that if she isn't scared or feeling upset before she addresses a group, "I don't do a very good job."

Eleanor McClinton, a United Church laywoman from Yellowgrass, Saskatchewan, whose association with Mary goes back to sharing a room at the United Church Training school, says being one of the early ordained women in the province had its burdens for Mary Haggart. "I think she has felt discrimination right from the very beginning, but has somehow learned to work with it and help people to perhaps accept the ministry by women, without doing it in an antagonistic type of way." Mary has always been able to help women understand the issues they face, says McClinton, but she doesn't make a big issue of it.

Women's concerns have, indeed, been one of her interests and inclusive language is important, says Mary. "But, I'm not willing to go overboard on it. I consider myself a liberated woman, but I don't think I'd call myself a feminist. I just think women should have a fair shake."

Mary served at Cabri for seven years, then moved to Balmoral United in Saskatoon for another five years. She preferred to stay in one place longer than three years because she believes a minister can't do very much in that time. "It takes that long for the minister to get to know the people, for the people to get to know the minister — to develop that kind of trust to enable them to work in committee and to find the leaders and draw them out and help them to be better leaders. One of the happiest experiences I have is when I see one of these leaders taking his or her place in presbytery or Conference and in the community," says Mary.

In 1966, Mary became the minister at Leask, 90 kilometres southwest of Prince Albert, Saskatchewan. She stayed there for six years. Her task was to bring the United and Anglican congregations together under one minister. "But, that didn't work out and we ended up changing the boundaries of the charge," she says.

While at Leask, Mary started an Alcoholics Anonymous group on the local Indian reserve and helped to counsel those in need. She also "inherited" some used clothing and had to figure a way to get it to those who needed it most, the native people who made up half her congregation, without having them feel belittled. So she helped organize a monthly rummage sale which raised money for the church, distributed the clothes and let the needy keep their dignity. "I never liked it when people gave me used clothing to wear when I was going to school," recalls Mary. "I realize how important a person's dignity is."

In 1972, Haggart moved to Central Butte, Saskatchewan, a community of 650 people about 90 kilometres northwest of Moose Jaw. She served the charge until her retirement in 1985, when she moved into a small cottage at nearby Riverhurst, overlooking Lake Diefenbaker and the South Saskatchewan River. It was in this charge that Mary's involvement in mission outreach really blossomed.

"When I arrived in Central Butte, there was an ecumenical Bible study group and through that I made a great number of friends who were not necessarily United Church people," she says. "It was out of that that we began to do seminars in an attempt to answer people's (mission) questions. One of the teachers there, Betty Payne, and I teamed up a lot and that's how we got involved in Ten Days (For World Development)."

The two women formed a very active Ten Days group. They had speakers come into the community and they organized projects which helped local people broaden their understanding of mission.

"We had a lot of fun," recalls Betty Payne of the years when Mary was most involved in Ten Days. The group, which ranged from 9 to 15 people, had study sessions, watched films and made meals from other countries. A food booth was set up in town once a week for three years at garden harvesting time to allow people to exchange surplus food items and learn something about Ten Days as well. "That extended to where people would bring children's boots and home baking. Nobody was supposed to pay for anything, but we couldn't stop people," says Payne.

"They did some very creative things," says Rev. David Petrie, a member of Saskatchewan Conference's program staff. "One year they produced their own tabloid for the Ten Days program in which they drew comparisons between the concerns for Nicaragua and concerns in Saskatchewan."

"That was one of the projects that was very exciting," says Payne. In the fall of 1982, local people were interviewed about various issues and excerpts were taken from publications in Saskatchewan and Central America. The four pages of newsprint tackled such concerns as what's changing for women in rural Saskatchewan and Nicaragua, what's being done for the elderly in each location, who will own the land and how do we stand in solidarity?

The paper was placed in all the mailboxes of Central Butte, Riverhurst, Eyebrow, Tugaske, Brownlee and Chaplin, says Payne. It was a project which captured the imaginations of Ten Days members and kept them working long into the nights.

Although no one really knows where some of the ideas for projects came from, Payne says Mary Haggart has been a major force within the group throughout her involvement. Mary continues that involvement today in her role as treasurer. Other pastors have been involved in the group over the years, but none for as long as Mary.

"The Ten Days group has become like a family," says Payne. "We're always there for each other. If you were doing something in your own church, you could count on the Ten Days people showing up," adds Payne, who is Catholic. "It was kind of a family and Mary had a position there of stability. Mary was, you could almost say, the mother figure and the gathering point. I think people felt she had a practical outlook, but also a spiritual outlook on what was going on."

"Mary challenged people to think," says Payne. "She didn't leave things on the surface." She would often ask, "But, why is it that way?"

When people in the community began losing their land, Mary made the connection between the agricultural problems and the resulting social changes such as alcoholism or people losing concern for their physical appearance. "It was a more whole look at people as people," notes Payne.

One of Mary's particular skills is making new people feel comfortable and encouraging everyone to use their gifts, says Payne. "She would remind us that we all had to work on the openness of the group. Mary would make a real effort, when somebody new came along, to stop the jargon and say things more clearly."

Bible reflection was done in a way that was non-threatening to non-church people. These people were invited to join in and often did. "She certainly raised the consciousness among United Church people and because of her interest and her commitment to it (mission) in all her work in the church, she broadened the perspective of people to the world view," says Payne.

This interest and commitment has led Mary to play many roles in her church. She was instrumental in forming the Rural Interchurch Development Education Project Co-op in Central Butte, which is an organization dedicated to building and maintaining a global justice network of volunteers in Saskatchewan. Mary was chair of Saskatchewan Conference in 1975 during the 50th anniversary of the United Church and a candidate for United Church Moderator in 1977. She chaired the Saskatchewan Conference Division of World Outreach from 1983 to 1986 and has attended the national Division's annual meetings many times. In 1984, she received an honorary doctor of divinity degree from St. Andrew's College in Saskatoon for her contributions to the life and work of the church.

Since 1984, Mary has been on the board of the Saskatchewan Council for International Co-operation, an umbrella organization that supports mission projects in developing countries. She has been actively involved in the animation committee of the national Division of World Outreach, working to make mission education and action more meaningful and important.

Mary's interest in mission energized the congregations under her leadership. She proudly says that the mission givings in each of the charges she served rose during her time there.

Mary has done considerable travelling across Canada in the last 30 years and she sees something new each time she crosses the country. "I guess life is an adventure. I'm still at it," she says with characteristic enthusiasm. But, her trips to other countries were what had the most impact on her world view and sense of mission.

In 1958, Mary went to a Sunday School convention in Japan and learned very quickly that the propaganda she had been taught while she was in the army was untrue. "We'd seen all these movies about the terrible Japanese people and learned (on this trip that) they're just ordinary folk like we are," she says.

In the late '70s, she travelled to Israel. "That had a profound effect on me, too, because it made the Bible become more alive," she says.

Then, in 1985, she used three weeks study leave to visit Central America. The experience is still vivid in her mind. "It was a very moving experience," she says slowly, "to meet mothers of the disappeared and people who were working for human rights; to see (in Nicaragua) what I had been hearing about and reading about for quite a few years; to meet people whose families... had been imprisoned and put to death." She recalls meeting "a fantastic person" in Nicaragua who was retired from teaching and had become a member of the militia "because no contra was going to enter her home."

Mary is passionate about aid to developing countries and her concern comes through when she talks about the need to help Central Americans help themselves.

"The thing that impressed me most was meeting the people

of the Christian base communities," says Mary. "It was out of these communities that the revolution was born... Nicaragua's Christian base communities grew from people who wanted to solve their own problems, so they prayed and looked for a way to overthrow dictator Anastasio Somoza." They succeeded in 1979, but "they're still struggling to get that revolution of theirs to work. If it works, that will mean that many of the countries in South America and Central America will be able to provide for their own and to share what they grow and make with others. I think that is a movement toward what we call a shalom, or the Kingdom of God."

Rev. David Petrie and Eleanor McClinton recall being at a Saskatchewan Conference DWO meeting just after Mary returned from Central America. "She arrived at the meeting out of breath," says Petrie. "She set a ceramic cup and saucer down on the table and said: 'I brought you this from Nicaragua.'"

"It was a clay cup that had been given to her to share with the people here," recalls McClinton. "I remember it being used at the communion service of that Division meeting." When you're in a developing country and come face to face with the people who are in need, "it's like a new conversion almost," says McClinton. Mary Haggart had come back from Nicaragua converted, or at least with a renewed sense of purpose.

Her mission has been to follow the leading of the Holy Spirit, says Mary. "We used to call it being obedient, but that's not well understood these days. It was never a blind obedience. It was always making a decision."

She wants "to tell the good news, to be a pastor and a friend, to love — even when they spit in your eye." It's a mission she couldn't get out of, she says. "There was no way to say no. I was being serious about what I believed and trying to do what the Spirit said to do."

It's also the mission she believes all Christians should have. "Our number one responsibility," she says, "is to tell the good news, the gospel of Jesus, in as many ways as we can, to nurture and encourage people who become Christians. I also think we must work for justice for all people and that means helping people to make their own decisions, supporting them while they learn how and enjoying their friendship."

The United Church is doing that in some ways, "but

sometimes we get so caught up in justice issues that we get out of touch with what God's spirit wills us to do." The inclusive language issue is one example. "Though it must be faced and we must do something about it, we must not lose sight of the fact that we are called to love one another as Jesus did."

On a local level, Mary says the United Church in Saskatchewan has to learn "how to interpret what we mean by 'the church'. Is it the coming together of Christians involved in ministry to one another? Is it the building on the corner, the place for weddings and funerals? Or is it the gathering and the going out of people involved in God's work?"

Her caring for people is apparent to anyone who has rubbed shoulders with Mary. There have been many funeral services which she has had to do from memory because she couldn't see through her tears. She recalls one experience of walking up to the house of a family whose teenage son had just been killed in a car accident. She had known and liked the boy a great deal herself. She heard crying coming from inside the house as she walked up the steps and she had to muster up her strength to knock. "I knocked on the door and I heard someone say, 'It's Mary.' And what a fantastic peace came into the house," she says.

Those are the experiences Mary would some day like to put down on paper — personal stories of mission.

Janet Graham got involved in the United Church and the Ten Days group at Central Butte because of the care Mary gave to her dying father. "My father had a great respect for her opinion on literature and he was interested in writing," says Graham. "She was very attentive to father..."

Mary Haggart has never married, although she was engaged to a man once. The reason for the break-up says a great deal about Mary's independent outlook. "He started telling me what to do and I figured that's not my cup of tea, so goodbye."

A persistent person who works hard for what she wants, Mary, nonetheless, has been unsure of herself many times. However, at those times, she has drawn on a greater strength. "I've always had that sense that, wherever I've been, whether it's joyful or sad or whatever, God is with me. And, I know there are lots of things I've done that I wouldn't be able to do otherwise," she says.

Once given a project, Mary will work endlessly to see it to completion, spending hours on research and writing. "She doesn't dabble," says Graham.

Mary is quick to accept a challenge, such as the one laid down many years ago by one of her university professors. That particular challenge set her on a life-long search. "The professor said, 'There is no God. You can't prove it.' And, that set me to digging," says Mary. "And, one could say I'm still digging, still working at an understanding." But, she doesn't have to *prove* God's existence to herself any more. "I just know," she says.

Mary has taken some unpopular stands over the years and her work with various parts of the church wasn't always appreciated by all the people in her congregations. "They thought she was spending too much time away from the charge," says Vi Torrie, an active United Church laywoman at Riverhurst and a long-time friend. "They expressed their views, but they never told her to stop it."

Certainly, not everyone was pleased with the issues Mary raised. When a coal-fired generating station was planned for the area, she got involved in examining the acid rain issue for Ten Days. She went on to voice her concerns for environmental safety in a Sunday sermon. Some people weren't very happy about that, says Graham. "The general attitude was that ministers should talk only about the Bible."

Mary seemed to give the church all she had, says Torrie. "I feel she still does, because I can never get hold of her," she adds with a laugh.

Mission in the church has changed considerably over the years, says Mary, and the changes are for the better. When she was a child, explaining the church's mission work involved showing children a slide show about the animals and people in other countries. "Gradually, we got so we told the stories of what the missionaries were doing and, once in a while, we met people from these countries. But, now, we're trying to say, 'This is what we're doing and this is why we're doing it.' It's gone all the way from the church doing for the poor, ignorant heathens over there to 'What can I do to help that person have a say in his or her way of life and perhaps meet that person as a brother/sister some time in the future?' "

Unfortunately, the average United Church person

doesn't have a sense of mission, says Mary. "But, there are members within the church, both lay men and women, who have a very strong sense of mission and some of them are looking for direction,"

The church itself has changed a lot since Mary entered the ministry in 1954. It used to be that everyone had to go to church and pastors wondered how many of those in the pews were committed Christians. Today, "about the only people that go are committed Christians," says Mary.

Looking to the future, Mary is unclear about some of her plans, saying she hasn't received her "marching orders" yet. But, she expects her involvement at the Conference level of the church to slow down somewhat. She'll always be active at the local level. "I'll always be a pastor and, if I ever get the hang of the computer, maybe I'll get the ideas out and print them. Maybe they'll become my memoirs. There are lots of stories to tell," she says.

For relaxation at home, Mary wanders along the shores of Lake Diefenbaker, paints landscapes and is "branching out, trying to learn how to sketch and do animals." She's a capable photographer and golfer, says Graham, which are two more hobbies this talented woman is going to pack into her retirement years.

There's no worry about Mary ever being bored, says Graham. "I think that's one word she hasn't found in her dictionary."

GERALD HANKINS:
DOCTOR ON THE ROOF
OF THE WORLD

by Gillian Snlatynski

At the top of the world, sandwiched between China to the north and India to the south, lies the little country of Nepal. The mountains of the Himalayas stretch across its northern border, including towering Mt. Everest, the world's tallest mountain.

The ruggedness of its mountain terrain — and a government which actively sought to restrict outside influences — kept Nepal isolated from the rest of the world until the 1950s. At that time, a change of government began to move the country into the twentieth century.

Development is now an important characteristic of Nepal. Roads and airports are being built, communications expanded, schools and hospitals established. But, the literacy rate is still only about 23 per cent in this country of 17 million people and its still fairly primitive health services must contend with diseases like leprosy and diphtheria, as well as the widespread health problems that come from poverty, lack of education and superstition.

In 1974, a Calgary doctor named Gerald Hankins arrived to work in a 140-bed hospital in Kathmandu, the capital of Nepal. The hospital was run by the United Mission to Nepal, an international, interdenominational mission involved in some 75 medical, educational and economic development projects in the country.

It wasn't Gerald's first visit to Nepal. He had come four years earlier as a two-month, temporary replacement for another doctor. In fact, he had first applied for medical missionary work in Nepal in 1959 — and been rejected.

When he arrived in 1974, a medical missionary at last, he was 50. He left behind a successful practice in specialty surgery and a solid professional reputation in Calgary. What he entered was a mass of Third World-type health problems that were, as he puts it, "way over my feeble head!" But, he stayed to deal with them for 12 years.

Gerald can't remember exactly when the seeds that bore fruit in Nepal were planted in his life. The path in front of him never seemed very clear. Certainly, as a boy, it didn't seem that his life would take the course it did.

He spent his early boyhood in Midnapore, now a Calgary suburb, which was a little village some miles out of the city in the 1930s. His mother was a single parent who depended on "relief" payments of $10 a month and the help of thoughtful neighbors to raise her two young sons. Times were very tough. "Those days make a deep impression on you. You never forget them," he says.

In 1936, the family moved into Calgary and Gerald started high school. His own assessment is that he was "no great shakes as a student." However, his academic ability won him a trip to Quebec in the summer of 1940, when he was 16.

"In those days," says Gerald, "for somebody from Alberta, it was, I suppose, an even grander adventure than it would be for people to travel to India and Nepal from here nowadays.

"And, to meet French-speaking people and to experience life in Quebec was a phenomenal experience — to find out that they were really pretty decent people, those French Canadians!"

That was also the summer when the Battle of Britain was at its height and Britain's survival seemed in doubt. They were dark, strange days to be planning a normal future.

He started university, anyway, aiming for an honours degree in modern languages. There was still very little money. A paper route helped a little— "With a paper route you can do marvellous things!" But, Gerald's interest in university studies was dwindling as fast as his funds. After a year, he gave up and took a "very uninspiring" job with Canadian Pacific Railways for nine months. Then, in January, 1942, "like everyone else," he joined up.

After 10 months' training, he was sent to England with the Royal Canadian Air Force where he got still more training as a navigator (using the newly-discovered radar technology). Then, with his squadron almost ready to be sent into action, Gerald was involved in an airplane crash just outside Edinburgh,

Scotland.

He was taken to hospital on November 7, 1943 with crush fractures of three vertebrae. "Not all that serious," Gerald claims, but enough to keep him hospitalized and in a cast for seven months. He was 20 years old.

"I was put in a body cast and I was lying in Princess Margaret Rose Hospital in Edinburgh feeling a bit sorry for myself.

"One of the most distressing parts of it all was the fact that my squadron, which had been training just outside Edinburgh, was about ready to be posted to the south of England for operations. It meant that those guys would go on without me. That was one of the hardships, to have your buddies leave you."

Into the hospital and up to his bed came a little Scottish woman named Mrs. Lynn. "She was a short little lady, perhaps in her 50s, and 'verra' Scotch. It's so long ago, I've forgotten the exact details. But, I know that under her influence I became a Christian . . .

"She became what I guess you would call my spiritual mother. There wasn't anything dramatic that happened. She just didn't give up. She didn't give up on me . . .

"She was kind of an old-fashioned believer. We don't disparage them now, but we look on them as a bit out of date. She moved at the impulse of the Holy Spirit — well, dear me, let's hope people still do that! The word she often used was 'impulse'. Whatever it is, it was an impulse that sent her up to the hospital that day. And, I subsequently went down to her house and drank tea and learned some of the basic tenets of Christianity. Of course, I had heard them in a casual way before, but here it was being focussed very clearly. I suppose we might call her a little overly fundamental. But, no one could doubt her sincerity."

Mrs. Lynn gave him a New Testament and wrote to him when he was sent to a convalescent hospital on the west coast of Scotland. He still has the letter she wrote to him when, out of hospital at last, he was headed for service in the Far East. She told him: "I shall be praying for you, that your faith fail not."

Gerald was stationed at a base just outside Calcutta and he was still in India for VE Day in May, 1945, and when the atomic bombs were dropped on Hiroshima and Nagasaki in August. The war was over.

"Everybody, but everybody, talked about getting back home . . . But, the question for many of us was, 'How on earth are we going to fit in?'"

For most people of his generation, the war was a watershed time and the end of the war meant new life. But, Gerald was returning to Canada having changed more, perhaps, than many of his peers. For one thing — significant, perhaps, in view of what came later — he had seen India. "The plight of that country — that left its mark, I think." But, most important, thanks to the spiritual nurture he had received from Mrs. Lynn, he had a new, strong faith.

"If our faith means anything to us, it should give us some cause for rejoicing, even if we're being shot at or bombed. We should still have some security not to be found elsewhere. I can honestly say that was true for me.

"When it comes to a question of deciding your future, some people say, 'I want to do God's will.' And, for some, it's almost as if there's a big arrow pointing out the direction, unmistakably. But, for most of us, it's not quite so easily discerned."

Like other returning veterans, Gerald heard of the government rehabilitation programs available in Canada. He thought he might use the promised gratuity to buy a small farm. But, before leaving England on the boat for home, he got some vocational counselling from an RCAF personnel officer who told him his test results indicated an aptitude for some sort of helping profession. He was advised to think about medicine and he took the advice seriously.

Back in Calgary, after three months of intensive cramming in chemistry, he joined a special class for veterans at the University of Alberta in Edmonton in January, 1946. He was "still in some doubt" that this was really God's will for him, but he immersed himself in the work anyway.

Also in January, 1946 — at a New Year's party — he met "a girl in a yellow sweater" who changed his life in another way. He married Alison Matthews of Calgary in June, 1948, with three years of medical study still to go.

Before their marriage, both had been part of a United Church congregation in Edmonton and they participated in the Student Christian Movement on campus. But, Gerald didn't have a home for his own Christian faith at that stage. "I didn't quite know where I actually fitted." Then, he and Alison went to Strathcona Baptist Church in Edmonton and they knew they'd found their place.

Both were baptized in December, 1949, by one of two men who were to have a profound influence on their growth as Christians. George Edwards was Strathcona's pastor — a "diamond in the rough." G. Fred McNally, chancellor of the University of Alberta, chaired the board of deacons at Strathcona. Both men were sources of friendship and spiritual support for Gerald and Alison. They probably had "every bit as much influence as Mrs. Lynn," says Gerald. "There was a kind of disdain for anything spiritual (on the part of) most of the professors and teachers in the faculty of medicine . . . We were taught that flesh and blood is all that matters. So I was very grateful for those other outside influences."

After graduation in 1951 and two years of internship, Gerald was becoming aware that his real interest was surgery. He was advised to return to England for graduate training.

In 1953, with a wife, three small daughters and little money, he arrived in London for a four-year stay. Study for the rigorous British fellowship exam was gruelling but, at the time, Gerald had no misgivings about his choice of career. "Medicine can be completely absorbing — maybe too absorbing. In fact, that's one of the real dangers. It can swallow you up, completely."

The family returned to Calgary in 1957 with a British-born son as well as the three small daughters. Right away, there were debts and the prospect of more debts to come. In the first month working at his own medical practice, Gerald earned $43.

"Things gradually built up. But, it wasn't very satisfying in a way because everything was estimated in terms of dollar bills . . . If I stay around all the time, I will get more phone calls and more work and earn more money and pay off my debts. But, what about the family? And, what about my surgical training? Isn't it worth anything? It was very demoralizing."

It was during this time, in 1959, that he heard of a need for doctors at a mission in Nepal. He and Alison applied through the Baptist Overseas Mission Board. They were turned down.

One reason for the rejection was that the Board's limited funds were needed for work just begun in Angola. There wasn't enough money to support missionaries in Nepal as well. The other stated reason was that the Hankins were considered "unsatisfactory missionary material." It was a blow, especially because there was no further explanation. However, says Gerald, the setback was "not insurmountable." His medical practice gradually built up and the debts were paid off.

At the same time, he worked on his church's board of deacons and taught Sunday School. It didn't feel like a new personal mission, but "I guess it was enough to capture my interest and attention for a few years."

Then, in 1962, Gerald was invited to join another doctor in Edmonton for further training in oncology (which concerns the treatment of cancer). Eighteen months later, he was back in Calgary with some highly specialized experience in the surgical treatment of cancer, particularly of the head and neck. That led to the establishment of a completely surgical practice.

"I was working as a consultant and that's really good for a person's feeling of self-esteem . . . And our kids were growing up and our financial status was improving."

Although earning a "nice fat salary" led to a certain amount of comfort and security, Gerald was aware of "never really feeling at ease or fulfilled by doing it." The idea of medical missionary work never went away.

In 1966, he took part in a two-week medical group mission to Mexico through the Christian Medical Society. "That was useful experience, to work in this deprived part of Mexico—doing nothing very valuable — what could you do in two weeks? But, we at least could see the problems and all of us who were there, I think, benefitted ourselves, even if we didn't benefit the local people."

At home during those years, he was able to take more time for his family. He and Alison became very involved in running wilderness camps for the Baptist Church. The camps brought together 35 children for a week at a time. Some of them were "really rough and tumble." But, all were exposed to the Christian message, albeit in a low-key style. One boy, whose language when he came to camp "would curl your hair," was later baptized in their church.

"You know, it's hard to measure these things," says Gerald. "You can't measure them. That might have been more important than working in Nepal for 12 years. Who's to say?

"I don't like to think that being a missionary is the ultimate in Christian service. . . . I don't believe that at all. I think it's just as important to be faithful in your own corner as it is to go across the world."

Who's to say that Gerald didn't finally win his dream by being faithful in his own corner? In 1970, he learned that the United Mission to Nepal (UMN) needed a doctor for two months to replace a medical missionary returning to Canada for an extended furlough. (The missionary, a former classmate from Edmonton, was Dr. Helen Huston, one of the senior medical missionaries in the United Church.)

Gerald was accepted for the job and he set off for Nepal — at some risk to his practice and with many questions about his fitness for the work.

Of the medical scene in Nepal, Gerald says, "I don't know whether I did more harm than good. There was so much that was strange and new and different in terms of diseases and problems." Of the mission scene: "I found out that missionaries are not bad people after all! I thought you kept them off at arms' distance because they were cold-blooded and fragile and a little sanctimonious. What a stupid idea! In fact, some of them were among the most congenial, hard-working, honest individuals you would meet anywhere."

In 1973, he heard there was a desperate need for a surgeon (who would do nothing but surgery) in a larger hospital run by the UMN in Kathmandu. Word had been passed to the United Church's Division of World Outreach (DWO) that Dr. Gerald Hankins was the man for the job.

Going to Nepal had to be a family decision and all winter the Hankins wrestled with it. Their three oldest daughters had already left the nest, but their son was still at home finishing Grade 12. By now, they also had a fifth child, a daughter born in 1968. Alison, who some years earlier had returned to university to complete a degree in education, was now working on a Masters degree in social work.

Finally, they decided in favor of Nepal, applied and were accepted by DWO. They reached Kathmandu in August, 1974. After a few months of orientation and language training, Gerald got down to work. "There certainly wasn't much of an overlap," he says. "The skills of a surgeon working in Calgary were not much use in Nepal and this was something I had to find out and wrestle with. I had to go through another period of learning — but that was a good experience. It was fascinating work. And, over the years, it remained so. It never became dull."

Undergirding the work was strong support and spiritual nurture from the mission. There were prayer groups, Bible study groups, sing-songs and meetings over meals. "One of the big strengths of working in Nepal was the fellowship within the mission. It was an international mission, an interdenominational mission — but with warm fellowship. That's what sustained many, many people, I think."

Nepal is a difficult place to "do mission" in the sense of evangelization. About 90 per cent of the population is Hindu and it's against the law to change religions or persuade anyone to change. Christian congregations exist and, in fact, are growing. But, perhaps because of this growth, Christian pastors are jailed regularly. UMN workers are unable to serve congregations, baptize or, indeed, "preach the Good News" in any way.

"Under these circumstances," says Gerald, "I guess it would be safe to say we had to be doers of the Word . . .Some people, those who knew the language well enough and who could understand people's needs, were able to give them Gospels and speak to them. I never did that— I couldn't do it. I didn't have it within me to do it. But, I felt that to be the best doctor I could under those circumstances was probably the most important thing of all — and pretty demanding at times. . .There was a two-and-a-half-year period when I was by myself having to cope with all the surgical problems, including emergencies — when it was sometimes pretty difficult to muster up the energy to do the work that needed to be done, day and night.

He also saw it as part of his job "to be gentle with people" and not to swear at nurses and junior doctors or throw instruments at them or otherwise give way to stress and fatigue in ways that damage others. "There is a temptation to do that at times, when somebody is kind of dim. And, there is a real place for patience . . . I guess there was many a time when I was a very poor example . . ."

The Hankins family made a four-year commitment to the mission. When they returned to Canada on furlough in 1978, their future was very undecided. It was a struggle to know whether to return. Finally, says Gerald, "there was a need and we were invited to go back and we went."

It was during his second term in Nepal that a brand new opportunity for service presented itself. Through a chance meeting in England with Dr. Maurice King, an authority on health care in developing countries, Gerald was invited to contribute to four volumes of a book on primary surgery for developing countries which Dr. King was editing. This was to be "a cookbook of surgery," dealing with the sorts of problems a primary-care doctor in any small hospital in India or Bangladesh or Malawi might come across.

Gerald had come across many of these health problems himself in Nepal and had searched the available medical literature for help. But, medical texts published in the West lacked the insights of first-hand experience and doctors with first-hand experience weren't writing about it.

From the end of 1979 until 1985, in what little spare time he could muster, Gerald wrote 23 chapters. "That was fun! It wasn't anything very brilliant. I was just more or less writing from experience. Luckily, I did have some journals — more relevant, but not very well written — that I could call upon and the experience we had in our own hospital and (I) put this together and came up with some simple management."

The writing project gave a new and sustaining purpose to his time in Nepal. But, by 1986, the chapters were written. Their youngest daughter had just finished high school in India and the time seemed right to come home. "I guess, to be honest, I was getting a bit tired of those long working days. Not that there wasn't still lots of interesting work. But — I don't know how to describe it — I was quite happy when the work came to and end . . .

"If we stayed there too long, we would be foreigners in Canada. In many ways, we sort of feel that we don't quite understand the society here. We probably are odd men out, so to speak—foreigners in our own society, strangers in our own home town. The time had come to be assimilated back into our own society."

The Hankins returned to Calgary in August, 1986. Since then, "it's been a time of ups and downs but, by and large, it hasn't been too bad. And, for me, the gratifying part is to have new and challenging work."

Gerald's new work is writing. But, this time it's not to teach doctors about surgery. It's to educate as many people as possible about "the strength and worth of Christian missions in our day." One current project is a biography of Dr. Helen Huston, for many years his colleague in Nepal.

"In the United Church (congregations) I've spoken to, I always got a warm welcome. But, I found that people were remarkably ill-informed in most cases about what was going on . . .Most of them, I think, were keen to learn and were grateful for what it was possible to tell them about Nepal and the work that was being done there. And, for many of them, it was quite a revelation . . .

"I would have to say that, generally speaking, Canadian church people feel that the problems they have in their own country are more than they can cope with, let alone getting involved with what's going on in Third World countries — that unemployment and the disruption of the environment and free trade and all those things are enough for them to contend with. And, maybe they are."

He speaks with respect and affection about the United Church's Division of World Outreach, which paid his salary and took care of the family's physical needs during their years in Nepal. He approves of the Division's focus on human rights and justice issues and its critique of government policies worldwide. At the same time, he profoundly believes that missionaries still have an important service and witness role to play both at home and abroad. "I think we're still called, there's still a call to go out and tell the Good News — not necessarily verbally, but in some way or another. There's still a need for us to go and offer what we might have in places where there's desperate need.

MAY KOMIYAMA: BEACON FOR THE ETHNIC CHURCH

by Keith Howard

Laughter bubbles from May Komiyama like artesian springs escaping the earth. When her laughter breaks the surface, it slides away, drawing attention neither to itself nor its source. It simply warms those within its embrace. Twinkling eyes speak of friendliness and acceptance. Without being intrusive, she is at once present and reserved, interested and concerned.

Who is May Komiyama? What is she like? When asked these questions, the expressions on her friends and co-workers match those of someone asked why the moon floats in the heavens or the grass grows green. It's wonderful that it happens, but more difficult to explain why. Eventually, the adjectives begin to spill out quickly and easily — open, friendly, patient, faithful, courageous, accepting, tough, a person of deep faith.

It testifies to the force of her personality that the adjectives, though accurate, don't capture the magnetic first impression of this petite woman, with streaks of grey running through her once jet-black hair. May Komiyama looks Japanese. She is a Japanese-Canadian. Without assigning it secondary importance, May Komiyama is also a Christian.

Born to Japanese immigrants in Vancouver, B.C., the middle child of four daughters and a son, May never considered herself Japanese. In fact, her life has been the story of how she learned to accept herself, her culture and her faith.

From the time of their birth, her father, Heiji Yamazaki, was concerned that his children be good Canadian citizens. He oversaw the learning of "proper English" and the enrollment in "Canadian" churches and schools: David Lloyd George Elementary, Point Grey Junior High and McGee Senior High. The family's Japanese heritage took a back seat. May grew up with something of "a superiority complex" with respect to other Japanese girls who, with their accents and cliquishness, would "just stand off in a corner, giggling by themselves." So convinced was she of her own unity with the dominant white culture that she never questioned why she, unlike all the other neighbourhood children, wasn't allowed to go to the closest public school, Maple Grove Elementary. It was only later in life that she was able to resurrect and join together key memories which revealed a larger pattern of racial discrimination.

Grade one provided the first test of her true status in the white British Columbia of the late 1920s. May, with other Japanese-Canadian children, attended the English-speaking school, but not in the regular grade one class. "I had to go to the basement of an old Anglican church for grades one, two and three." The Parents-Teachers Association contended that allowing the Japanese to go into grade one with the rest of the children hindered the promise of the white students. The association assumed the Japanese-Canadian children couldn't speak English. In fact, May and her sisters spoke English in the home and "never could speak Japanese well." Still, life goes on, especially for children.

A staunch Methodist since before his immigration from Japan, the senior Yamazaki was equally diligent about his children's church attendance. Every Sunday morning, father and mother would drop May, her brother and three sisters off at the white Canadian Memorial congregation and then proceed themselves to the Japanese-speaking church. The result, says May, was that "my father so brainwashed me to believe I was Canadian that I really thought I was white. I just never thought of myself as Japanese."

World War Two and the evacuation of Japanese-Canadian citizens forced May to re-examine her nineteen years as a Canadian and as a Christian. She traumatically discovered that "I wasn't who I thought I was." The details seem simple in outline but horrific in reality.

At 7:55 a.m., December 7, 1941, Japan attacked Pearl Harbour, sinking or damaging 19 ships and killing 2300 people. The next day, Canada declared war and began the process of removing people of Japanese ancestry from the West Coast. Less than a month later, May Yamazaki, on the edge of fulfilling a life-long dream, entered Vancouver General Hospital to train as a nurse. Her total immersion in studies blocked any connection between herself and the war. But, six weeks after her entrance, at the end of February, 1942, she was given "three hours notice to get out of residence." Her family was being evacuated.

The Yamazakis were one of the "lucky" Japanese families who managed to keep their family unit together. May's sister, a public health nurse, went to work in Kaslo, B.C. and brought the family there.

The grief caused by the evacuation and the loss of her training was tempered by May's trust and hope in the rest of the nation and the church. "I wrote to every province in Canada, except Prince Edward Island, to try to find a hospital that would accept me." The United Church of Canada had a hospital at Lamont, Alberta. She expected acceptance and received denial. "They were the first hospital to reject me. That was more than a bitter blow to take because I really didn't expect our United Church hospital to turn me down."

The rejection, combined with the evacuation, led to a crisis of faith. "I went through quite a terrible stage of trying to hang onto my faith, but losing it." All through the war, "my father kept maintaining, 'There is a God, he still loves you and don't have any concerns about whether there's a God or not.' "

But, May didn't share her father's perspective. "I thought I just had the most stupid father in the world. How could he still say there is a God in light of all this? At the same time, I tried to hang onto my faith because, when I saw his was so strong, I thought there had to be something to it — but I sure didn't know what it was."

The silence of the institutional church intensified the pain. "They just kept quiet." Only isolated individuals spoke out against Prime Minister Mackenzie King's policy of forced reloca-tion of Japanese-Canadians. Only a few complained about the confiscation and auctioning of Japanese-Canadian property. May cites the story of Takashi Komiyama, her future husband, as a clear example of institutional indifference.

A graduate of Union College in Vancouver, Takashi Komiyama was ordained as a United Church minister by British Columbia Conference in 1942. "He had to have an RCMP escort to his ordination," says May, "because there was a curfew on us. No one was allowed on the street half an hour after sunset."

The church promised the Canadian-born Komiyama, who wasn't fluent in Japanese, that he wouldn't be sent to a Japanese-speaking area. But, "they didn't even honour that. They sent him to a place where there were 99 per cent Buddhists." Lemon Creek was a cow pasture converted to a shanty town to house the Japanese-Canadian evacuees. When the nearby white congregation at New Denver recognized Komiyama's gifts and asked that he be allowed to serve them as well, B.C. Conference agreed. However, says May, Conference made the stipulation that "he could not conduct any of the sacraments. He could do it for the Japanese people—that was OK," but not for the whites.

May's sense of abandonment by the corporate church is matched by her appreciation of individuals within the church. "I can't say enough how wonderful certain individuals were as individuals."

Etched most deeply in her memory are those who helped pick up the pieces of her nursing dream. A former missionary, Florence Bird, convinced the hospital in Guelph, Ontario to admit two oriental girls for training. May was one of them.

For May, the return to nursing was a pivotal event. "Looking back," she says, "it does seem that God has been directing my way." Her enrollment into training was just the first step. "From the very day I arrived, there was a message for me inviting me to spend my first weekend off visiting Dr. Flora Little." May knew nothing of Dr. Little or her mother, Margaret Gauld. A stranger in Guelph, May accepted the invitation. The warmth and acceptance they showed was a glimmer of light for a confused and hurting young woman far from home. Margaret Gauld, a missionary to Formosa at the turn of the century, provided May with a ready-made grandmother. "I was told this was my home and I was to go there whenever I wanted."

At first, May took the graciousness and hospitality for granted, feeling "this was how all Christians should act." Then, by chance, she learned that the Gaulds were carrying burdens of their own. One of their daughters, a missionary in Formosa, hadn't managed to get out of the country when war broke out. "When trying to escape from the Japanese, her plane was shot down. She was one of the few survivors, but they [the Gaulds] didn't know where she was and thought that she was lost." Eventually, the daughter was rescued and she managed to get back to England. What struck May with such force was that, though the Gauld's pain and anxiety "was all at the hands of the Japanese soldiers, they still made me just so welcome and treated me as one of their own!"

The Gaulds' faith and state of grace initiated the major turning point in May's life. "How could they still look on me and love me?" Her answer to that question shaped her view of God, her attitude towards others and her sense of her own mission.

In the midst of her faith crisis, May articulated her struggle as questions about God. How could a loving God permit such suffering? Why doesn't a God, reputed to be "love", reward the good and punish the evil? Then, in the love and care of the Gaulds, she glimpsed something more. "It was a big revelation to me to realize that this was what the Christian spirit of loving your neighbour was all about." Faith began to sprout, nurtured by the warmth and love of a family who "hated to be thought of as doing Christian acts" but who lived their faith completely— who went to church, but whose belief was expressed more in action than words.

May's vision of God expanded. She now talks of a God who transforms. "God really tries to make the best of the messes we humans make." This hard-won hope keeps her alert for the good in her own life, her family and an often indifferent and dozing church. "This is one of the main reasons I've been able to accept a lot of things which the church does not react to in a Christian way. It's not the faith that's at fault, it's the human element in it."

May Komiyama prefaces everything she says about the Canadian government's evacuation of its Japanese-Canadian citizens by noting that everyone's experience varied, even within her own family. There are no generalizations. The same perspective informs her view of faith. "Everyone has to come to grips with what their faith means to them."

May's faith is in a God who cares, who guides, who loves unconditionally and calls disciples to love their neighbours unconditionally. Her God also brings low the lofty, calling them to use their gifts responsibly. For May, the lessons didn't come quickly but, once learned, they've never been forgotten. She confesses readily to a sense of superiority in her early life. The war dealt a major blow to that image and the finishing touches were struck by her marriage.

After graduation from Guelph, May went to work in the public health system in Toronto. Takashi Komiyama, after his work at Lemon Creek and New Denver during the war, went to Montreal. Though they had always known each other— their fathers were schoolmates in Japan— their paths didn't cross again until eight years after their experiences in the B.C. internment camps. One summer, Tak, as May called him, was on holiday and honouring an invitation to be guest speaker at the Yamazaki's church in Toronto. May's father led the service and the guest preacher was invited home for lunch. In the afternoon, Tak proposed and May accepted. In the evening, they informed their parents. May's father, much to his daughter's embarrass-ment, responded to the announcement with a ten-minute lecture to the young preacher about the necessity of founding a marriage on "good Christian principles."

Earlier in her life, May had shunned the Japanese language. But, by the time she arrived in Montreal, a new bride and a minister's wife, things were different. "I really, sincerely began to feel sorry that I couldn't speak the language and that I couldn't feel more at one (with Tak's Japanese congregation). I felt the language barrier constantly with me and I really did try hard to overcome that. The first two years of my married life I didn't speak a word to any of the members of his congregation because I was so sure I would make a mistake or make a fool of myself.

"I had to start learning to converse with them and, in so doing, I gradually began to feel more at one with them. Some-where along the line— it was such a gradual process that I really don't know where it happened— I really saw how wrong I was to have that feeling of superiority and I felt more committed. I wanted to work with them and do what I could. After my husband died, people said to me, you should give up your membership in the Japanese congregation and go back to Canadian Memorial. But, I just couldn't bear doing that anymore."

May's solidarity with the ethnic church is unshakeable and has grown beyond the Japanese United Church she now attends in Vancouver. All ethnic congregations have become her special concern, whether they be Korean in Montreal, Chinese in Halifax or Japanese in Vancouver. Every opportunity, from being one of B.C. Conference's General Council representatives to chairing the national ethnic committee of the Division of Mission in Canada, is seized to promote further understanding and commitment between the growing ethnic communities and the shrinking white church.

May's work arises out of her appreciation for the gifts and shortcomings of these congregations and the larger church. She straddles both sides of the ethnic track and is convinced that "everybody has particular gifts to offer and that we are obligated to use those gifts."

The ethnic communities often "feel small and unrelated to the larger church." Their need is to feel part of The United Church of Canada. "Some find it pretty difficult to get over the fact that the Home Missions Superintendent is no longer there to be a father to them." As chair of the national ethnic committee, May encourages the ethnic churches to expand their vision of what they can be and do. "I'd like to help them enlarge their sights, to see how they can be a witness and offer their gifts to the United Church."

The rest of the United Church badly needs to be awakened from its slumber. "Canada is going to be over 50 per cent non-white people in a few years," says May, "and, if the United Church wants to survive, we're going to have to do something about learning to accept the rest of the people in the community as brothers and sisters, and to be really sincere about it."

May constantly works to increase visibility and awareness of ethnic concerns, particularly with those who can conceive only of a white church. She is often working to fight misperceptions about ethnic congregations. Presbyteries, in particular, worry about small ethnic congregations becoming too big a drain on their mission support grants. But, ethnic churches don't all remain dependent. "The Koreans are just fantastic at getting on their feet in a very short period of time. So (also) with the Chinese..." In contrast to many "established" congregations, ethnic congregations often have an abundance of vital young families. More often than not, says May, the United Church "is way behind in offering the hand of friendship and getting them going."

The church's future may well rest with the ethnic communities, but spreading that word proves very difficult. The head literally aches from running up against the proverbial brick wall too many times. People, often polite, don't always have much time for a little Japanese-Canadian woman and the concerns she represents.

What keeps May going, one more time, up the hill of indifference, is a deep sense of call, a sense of gift and obligation.

"God is up there looking after me and as long as I've got work to do here, I'll do it. I just hope I'll be able to read the proper directions— even though it sometimes takes several years before I wake up."

Though much of the help she has received during the very tough times of her life have come from Roman Catholics and Roman Catholic institutions, she remains, to the core, United Church. Her hope for her church seems both simple and profound.

"I hope that everybody can get to the point where they really see people as people. One of the ways that that would show to me is if, just off the street, people would come to our Japanese English-speaking congregation— and would feel that they'd like to become a member of our church, and work for us, and become part of us. That, to me, would be living proof. This is what the white church expects ethnic people to do, but I want to know why white people can't do the same thing?"

May Komiyama's life tapestry has taken on something of a circular pattern. She now lives with one of her two daughters, a son-in-law and a granddaughter on Laburnum Street in Vancouver. It's the same street on which she was born and raised, though the modern oak and brass elegance of her new home contrasts with the little house provided to her father, a gardener, by his wealthy employer. May, like her father, bypasses her childhood church, Canadian Memorial, to attend Vancouver Japanese United Church, confident in both her ethnic heritage and her ability to carry forward a vital Christian ministry.

As she has for so many years, May Komiyama continues to wrestle with and tenaciously love the United Church— the source of much pain and desolation in her life— but also the home of her faith and her faith's work.

STEPHANIE LYNN: QUESTIONER, SEEKER, DOER OF THE WORD

by Rhoda Playfair Stein

On a yellow-dust-blowing day in September, 1987 Stephanie Jane Lynn climbed a steep hill on Jordan's West Bank above Jericho. With fellow members of a Canadian Council of Churches fact-finding tour, she peered into the depths of a rocky ravine hundreds of feet below.

"The wind was blowing so hard I was clutching a huge stone cross for anchorage," she recalls. "I looked down into what seemed forever and the single thing in sight was St. George's Monastery, clinging to barren rock the way it had done for a thousand years. I was so overwhelmed I just let go and threw my arms into the air!"

That small incident offers a clue to the deep feelings and sensitivities that go along with being Stephanie Lynn. That, and her poignant observation: "As we drove away afterwards, I saw a sign on the fence that said, 'This is a military zone!' "

What was so young a woman (she was 19 at the time) doing on a Middle East delegation sponsored by the Canadian Council of Churches? Stephanie explains it as part of "the process" — the ongoing stream of events and happenings that have shaped her life to date.

In 1983, she attended her first youth conference at British Columbia's Naramata Centre and became a youth representative for Vancouver South Presbytery. "Things snowballed from there," she says. She became involved with youth work at the B.C. Conference level, attended the 1984 General Council in Morden, Manitoba and was asked to participate in Youth Forum when General Council met at Sudbury in 1986. Subsequently, she became chairperson of the B.C. Conference Youth and Young Adult Working Unit.

That was "the process" that led to her being chosen as the only youth member on the delegation, she explains.

This process, of course, didn't begin at Naramata. Stephanie was born into a deeply-committed Christian family (her mother, Patricia, teaches music, her father, Rodney, is a mathematics professor at the British Columbia Institute of Technology). She grew up on B.C.'s Lower Mainland but moved to Kenya when she was 11, where her father was employed on a water development project with the Canadian International Development Agency. Her four-and-a-half years in East Africa were both broadening and stultifying. They were broadening because she got intimately acquainted with another land and culture; stultifying because she spent two years at a mission school where her faith perspective was questioned, challenged and denied by the fundamentalist, right-wing style of Christianity on which the school was based.

"I got in trouble a lot," she recalls with a little-girl grin. "Mostly around boy/girl relationships — you got a demerit for things like holding hands or being in a non-lit area with any male. I had enough demerits to get suspended but, as I was president of my class, they let it go." There were positives as well as negatives attached to the school. It was wonderful to be among people her own age — and it was here she began to develop her leadership skills.

But, the Kenyan experience created problems of which Stephanie was acutely aware when she returned with her family to Canada in 1983. As a member of a mainline church (Gilmore Park United in Richmond, B.C.) she found herself among people whose expression of faith was much more subdued and low-key than what she was accustomed to in Kenya. "It was a constant battle for me," she recalls. "I think I was a difficult member of the congregation. I kept challenging people in my brash, 15-year old way and nobody was able to deal with where I was coming from."

Her frustration stemmed from her attempts to reconcile the two examples of Christianity with which she had been confronted: the narrow, fundamentalist model that she'd found oppressive because the world in which people live and function was portrayed as negative and hated by God ("That wasn't my experience of the world and I didn't want it to be") over against the mainline United Church model with its different words, symbols and value judgments.

At this point, it would have been easy enough to throw the whole church experience over, as so many of her teenage peers had done. But Stephanie isn't one to give up so easily. The strong, naive faith that had developed during her school years, coupled with the theology she had accepted almost subconsciously, had to be reckoned with.

Gradually, she became more and more appreciative of the United Church's stance with regard to people and the world in which we live and function as Christians. "It connects our understanding of God with the world — and that's what I'd been missing in the Christian environment presented at the school," she points out. While she found it frustrating that people within the church patronized her as a young person, there were also those who encouraged her and presented role models which permitted her to stay and grow and feel close to the United Church as a body of people.

The Middle East trip broadened her horizons in all directions. It was undertaken at the invitation of the Middle East Council of Churches with the intent that the Canadians would bring greetings, try to understand what was happening in the Middle East and take back their findings to Canadian church groups. It was an amazing experience for a young person to be one of two United Church members (a former Moderator, Very Rev. Bruce McLeod was the other) on a 12-member delegation that included Quakers, members of the Coptic, Greek and Armenian Churches in Canada, the Orthodox Church in America (Canada) as well as mainline church representatives.

Making the connection between the history of Christianity in the Middle East and the contemporary situation of those now living there strengthened Stephanie's resolve to work with people on an international level. "I always knew from my junior high days in Kenya that I wanted to do international relations," she says. With this in mind, she's majoring in anthropology at the University of British Columbia. "I want to be able to relate internationally and to help others relate internationally and I can do that most effectively through anthropology."

Her choice of anthropology rests on the fact that it focuses on being able to see people from their own perspective, apart from a cultural, religious or economic bias. Through its study she feels she'll develop analytical skills that will help her understand international relations by creating a sense of what's actually happening in as true a way as possible.

Out of this interest in international relations has grown Stephanie's concept of her mission in the church. "I see myself as being an enabler," she says firmly. "Enabling groups of people to come together." That could happen for her by means of organizations such as the United Nations or the World Council of Churches, but wherever it happens it will involve God and Christ. "My life is a process — and God is inextricably a part of that. When I'm talking about mission, I'm talking about how my faith expresses itself in concrete terms as I relate to the world. My mission has to be an extension of myself."

Among other things, the Middle East trip deepened that faith relationship with God and the world. On a day to day level it was exhausting, mind-stretching and gut-wrenching. Seven of the 12-member group (including Stephanie) spent the bulk of their time in Syria while the remainder of the group went to Lebanon.

Their days began in the morning at 6:30 and ended in the evening at 11:30. The 17 hours in between were crammed with meetings and luncheons at which they spoke with Jews, Muslims, Christians, local government officials, U.N. peace-keeping force members and political leaders. In addition, there were trips arranged by their hosts and dinners with embassy staff members.

One of the most moving events, etched with acid on Stephanie's brain, occurred during their two-and-a-half day visit to Egypt. Described in her own words, a stark picture emerges: "We were dressed in our best to meet Pope Shenouda III, Patriarch of the Coptic Orthodox Church. He's a charming, charismatic person whom we enjoyed meeting but immediately afterwards, dressed up as we were, we were taken to view a church project intended to improve standards of health and education within a garbage collectors' village.

"As we arrived in Mo'Attamidya, a village of 11,000 people, the horse-drawn garbage collecting carts were also arriving. Dust flew everywhere. From 4 a.m. until noon, men and children had been collecting garbage for which they receive income and now their carts were backed into the living rooms of their houses and dumped. The women and children sort after that. What's recyclable is set aside and the rest is put into a heap by the front door and burned.

"We went through the building that housed the project and then were taken into one of the houses where the villagers lived — a lean-to really — with a living room, a bedroom and a room for the pigs.

"The most horrible thing for me was the feeling that everything, including the people around me, was not clean. We shook hands and I wanted to wash myself. The smell was over-powering. I watched a baby crawl onto a garbage pile, pick up a rotten orange and put it in his mouth. All the children were very sick. Everyone suffers from belharzia, a water-borne disease. Their water source, sewage outlet and swimming pool are one and the same.

"One of the most awful parts was being so dressed up! To make things worse, we were driven straight to the Intercontinental Hotel after the village encounter for a seven-course dinner with Egypt's minister of immigration. The contrast was incredible! But, that's what it was like to be a member of the delegation."

For Stephanie, the entire 15-day experience was overwhelming. Just being there as a youth delegate and having the amount of credibility she had never been given as a 19-year-old student — being considered a VIP for six to seven hours at a time for instance — was a tremendous experience. She began asking herself how she could organize the complexity of it all so she could communicate it to people in Canada.

Actually, Stephanie had already begun that organization during the course of the trip. She somehow found time to take copious notes, concluding that the most apparent areas of concern were poverty, health, education, militarism, violation of human rights and peacekeeping.

She puts her key learnings into three groups. First, is the interconnectedness of people. "What we do and say in Canada affects people in the Middle East because it affects economic and political decisions. We can choose to be educated about the real situation or to ignore it — but if we choose education, we must do something for peace and justice in our world."

Secondly, Stephanie learned that the Middle East was more important than she had ever imagined. "We hear so little, we tend to underestimate the importance of what happens there — yet so many things that affect the world community occur in that area."

Thirdly, she felt strongly that while there was a time for being a delegation and talking, there must also be a time for action — of working together over an extended period of time. "I had this sense of talking, talking, talking — for 15 days!" After a point, that became frustrating and she felt a need for people to become involved with one another in a working relationship. "I came to see the need for both talk and action."

Talk and action. For Stephanie, it's all tied together in the *process.* She works within the United Church structure because that's where she sees herself growing and enabling at this point in her life, specifically through her work with the Youth and Young Adult Working Unit in B.C. There, she sees an opportunity to create awareness and broaden the understanding of international concerns.   Stephanie's motivating force is her faith, which she describes as "almost an aspect of my personality in the same way, say, that I'm a loving or happy person." In a way, she says, that statement maintains that faith is a product of one's history and environment. Where there are examples of faith, one is taught to be faithful.

Certain incidents that influenced Stephanie's faith flare like beacons in her memory. One occurred in a sixth grade mathematics class in Canada. From her earliest years, she had somehow been convinced that people are equal and that conviction was underlined one day in class during a study of fractions. The teacher ("an understanding, sympathetic man who allowed us to develop at our own pace, make mistakes and not be embarrassed") had drawn two pies on the board. They were the same size and shape but they were divided into a different number of pieces.

It was one of those moments when, in a lightning flash, new understanding was born. "I realized those pies were the same as people," she recalls. "Just as each pie was divided into a number of pieces that made up the whole, each person is made up of different abilities, strengths and experiences that complete the whole person.   As a grade nine student in Kenya she had a vivid realization that she could have a personal, growing, friendship-relationship with Christ. "And that was an awesome and glorious realization! It was a real turning point for me; something to call upon for strength and joy." That realization has happened again and again, she declares, like her West Bank experience the day she climbed the hill above Jericho.

Does Stephanie Lynn see herself as an evangelist? She ponders the question carefully before answering. "Christ is very real and central for me and I'm willing to share that, but I don't feel that my experience is right for everybody. If that's evangelism, I'm an evangelist."

Her personal mission fits with what she considers to be the local and global mission of the church: to create an awareness of needs and an environment in which those needs can be met. One part of that mission calls for the creation of a real community so that risking, in the form of talking about and facing up to needs, can happen in a supportive atmosphere. She's convinced that any faith must be lived in a community and feels the United Church is beginning to understand that community must be interdenominational.

Stephanie is disturbed that so few lay people are involved with mission. It's always the same people who are involved and working, she points out. She has a distinct feeling that many in the pew feel cut off from mission involvement because they feel various care groups have presbytery, Conference or General Council status and, therefore, must be difficult to enter. They also note the immense amount of commitment given by those who are involved and feel unable to commit themselves to that extent. "That alienates many people who would like to become involved. I think we need to work on that as a church."

Stephanie is shrewd enough to observe, however, that while there are those who feel alienated by structure, there are many who are not in sympathy with the church's mission and don't want to be involved. "Perhaps that's because, when we look at the needs of people locally or globally, our own situation is called into question. That makes it very risky. The implication is that we may have to give up something; that hanging onto our lifestyles is not as fair or just or peace-loving as we've thought."

Part of the difficulty may lie with the fact that we're not an international church. As The United Church of Canada we tend to look at problems from a national perspective and see only Canadians.

The international links are there, of course. Through them, Stephanie believes, we've seen a new sense of mission develop over the years that has done away with the old concept of a superior society converting the heathen. At the same time, she feels the church is developing a sense that it must create a new environment in which we'll learn from one another and grow in a positive direction through international contacts.

Closer to home, in the four years she has been involved with youth work, Stephanie has noted many changes in attitudes. Where people used to feel comfortable saying negative things about youth, for instance, they no longer do that or they'd be embarrassed if they did. A positive concept of the young adult's place in the church is becoming accepted.

While involvement with church and university absorbs much of her time, Stephanie's hobbies offer recreation and a rounding out of her life. She's fond of dancing, music ("all kinds — I used to play French horn and piano, but have no time now") and reading. She's an ardent squash player and confesses to a love of skipping rope. In the near future she hopes to take a summer off and study French, realizing from her Middle East experience that as a Canadian she's expected to be bilingual.

Her friends, like herself, are open, seeking young people who are looking for answers to such questions as: What allows people to be violent? How can a religion based on peace be sustained solely by war? Why does a species like the human race propel itself toward self-annihilation? "We're overwhelmed by a sense of what we have to work with," says Stephanie. "There are so many problems. We are in danger of destruction from so many angles. We have to develop new skills to deal with it all because nothing like it has happened in the past."

The current depression among young people is due to the knowledge that they're not going to live as well as their parents and that has to do with a lack of faith in the system. Stephanie doesn't see this as expressing itself in a sixties-type, anti-system protest but, rather, as almost an exhaustion — a sense that the only way to handle things is to hope when there really isn't any room for hope.

That reflects the feelings of Stephanie's peers. However, with younger teenagers, the 13 and 14-year-olds, she notes a difference: a strong attachment to the status quo, to preserving the way things are. With a flash of her little-girl smile she quips, "They're almost like 13-year-old yuppies!"

However, says Stephanie, these things are true of young people only in North America. In Third World countries young people are much more radical, willing to risk their lives to change the system. What she sees here among the young and, in some instances, the not so young, is apathy and that frightens her more than anything else. "I don't know how to cope with that."

There is no naive, happily-ever-after expectancy in Stephanie's future but there is abiding hope. She sees herself working in her chosen field, making changes in her style and places of work as opportunities present themselves and somehow fitting that all together with marriage and a family down the road.

But, that's the future. For the present, she admits with endearing honesty, "I certainly haven't got things all sorted out yet."

Still, she's committed to the sorting and, in spite of her frustration with fundamentalist concepts, she remains suspended between two worlds. The United Church has a lot to learn from fundamentalism, she maintains. "We live our faith through our heads instead of our feelings and that's a loss. To understand and experience joy, glory, suffering, we have to see God as part of them. There must be a connection between the experiential and the world."

Stephanie Jane Lynn is earnestly seeking that connection in The United Church of Canada. It's imperative that she find it.